Self-Working

A Novel and Integrative Approach to Psychotherapy

Reza Johari Fard

Designer and Founder of Self-Working Psychotherapy

Serial Number: P2536130292
Title: Self-Working
Sub Title: A Novel and Integrative Approach to Psychotherapy
Author: Reza Johari Fard
Editor: Raha Ghafour Pour
Layout: Narges Taj
Cover Design: Ronya Johari Fard
ISBN: 978-1-77892-318-0
Subjects: Personal Growth, Applied Psychology
Format and Size: Paperback, 6 by 9 Inches
Pages: 136
Publication Date: February 2026
Publisher: Kidsocado International Publishing
Printed in the United States of America
Available in ebook editions.

Kidsocado International Publishing
Vancouver, Canada

Phone: +1 (236) 333-7248
WhatsApp: +1 (236) 333-7248
Email: info@kidsocado.com
Website: https://kidsocado.com
Address: 2100-1055 West Georgia St,
Vancouver, BC V6E 3P3, Canada

Dedicated to my teachers,

who taught me

knowledge,

and to my family,

who taught me

love.

Table of Content:

Preface

Over the past century, psychotherapy has witnessed the emergence of diverse approaches, each emphasizing specific aspects of human experience—from the unconscious and inner conflicts to cognitions, emotions, and interpersonal relationships. With the proliferation of these approaches, the need for theoretical and practical integration has become increasingly evident. The movement of Psychotherapy Integration formally emerged in the 1980s, aiming to overcome the limitations of single-school models (Norcross & Goldfried, 2005).

Despite of efforts, the central challenge remains: how can we provide a model that is theoretically coherent while simultaneously addressing multiple dimensions of human experience? To address this gap, the Self-Working model is proposed as a novel approach.

My familiarity with systems thinking, with its holistic, relational, and synthetic approach as opposed to detail-oriented and reductionist, and by taking into account the cultural context, led me to adopt a new approach to treating my clients, so that while analyzing and treating the individual's past, attention is paid to looking to the future and constructing the individual's specific narrative and path of his or her life, and most importantly, using the time and power of the present, a method that will position the individual for growth and development until the end of his or her life. Therefore, self-working is a therapeutic educational program based on recognizing and analyzing the individual's past and personality (Being-on-This), creating and constructing the future (Becoming-to-That); and moving along the path of life in the present time (Life Theme).

More than five years have passed since the first self-working books were designed and written in the form of test versions, and during these years, dozens of editing and rewriting of these books based on quantitative and qualitative research and various studies have brought self-working from a newborn to a dynamic, developing and gradually mature child, with much empirical evidence showing its effectiveness. This book, which is being published for the first time, is the result of these years of research and workshop training and studies of the effectiveness of its theoretical and technical sections. This book, along with the self-working workbook, can provide a comprehensive version of the introduction of this therapeutic approach and a new attitude towards life for therapists and clients.

This book, entitled "Self-Working A Nonel and Integrative Approach to Psychotherapy," is part of a self-working research project that has been studied for years in the form of experimental and therapeutic research in universities and clinical settings and is gradually being published. Many researchers and students participated in the implementation of this major research project, to whom I sincerely thank, and I hope that all interested parties and experts will send their comments to rjoharifard@gmail.com.

Reza Johari Fard
Psychotherapist-Assistant Professor
2025

Chapter 1

What is psychotherapy?

Chapter 1
What is psychotherapy?

The term psychotherapy is derived from the Greek root "psyche", meaning the life-giving soul and therapeia, meaning the servant or attendant of the soul (Tick, 1992). There are many definitions for psychotherapy, but here we will limit ourselves to a relatively comprehensive and practical definition. In general, psychotherapy is the conscious and prescribed application of clinical techniques and methods that are the result of the principles and theories of psychology, and specialists who have established therapeutic relationships with clients are engaged in this work to achieve the intended goals of psychotherapy in a way that is desirable for the client" (Johari Fard, 2024).

A simpler and more practical definition for psychotherapy is that, if we consider mental disorder as dis-order, meaning disorder and disorganization in the organization of the mind, then psychotherapy is in-ordering or, in other words, organizing the different parts of the mind, such as regulating the behavioral part with behavioral therapy, the cognitive part with cognitive therapy, emotions with analytical and emotion-oriented approaches, etc. (Johari Fard, 2024).

General Goals of Psychotherapy

Psychotherapy includes many approaches and systems, each of which will have different goals. However, behind this diversity, common goals can be listed as follows:

- Eliminating, changing, and stopping existing symptoms of the disorder,
- Intervening in abnormal psycholological patterns,
- Strengthening and developing positive aspects of personality,
- Modifying lifestyle,
- Emphasizing education and skill training,
- Emphasizing quality of life,
- Paying attention to the role of philosophical and semantic dimensions in health (Procheskaunorkras, 2018; Shamloo, 2002; World Health Organization, 2000).

Common Principles of Psychotherapy

At first glance, the various methods of psychotherapy seem very diverse and scattered together. However, with a methodological and clinical perspective, we can find that there are common principles in the theoretical and philosophical backgrounds and specific terminology of each of these approaches. Some of these common principles include:

1. Therapeutic Relationship

It is a conscious feeling of agreement, empathy, and mutual responsiveness between two or more people, with an emphasis on honesty, unconditional positive regard, and genuine empathy on the part of the therapist in this relationship (Kaplan & Sadock, 2023).

The therapist can use the following recommendations to create an effective therapeutic relationship:

- Be clear about what you want to convey to others.
- Consider your own and your audience's perspectives.
- Assess communication styles.
- Try to be clear and concise.
- Make sure the message is understood before continuing.
- Try to understand the audience's frame of reference.
- Express ideas in the simplest terms possible.
- Clearly define the audience's growth and development path.
- Express only one idea at a time.
- Take only one step at a time (have one goal).
- Use appropriate repetition to ensure understanding of the message.
- Compare ideas and highlight their differences.
- Use metaphors and similes.
- Emphasize fundamental ideas.
- Use language that engages all the senses.
- Use body language in harmony with the verbal message.
- Encourage and pay attention to verbal and nonverbal feedback.
- Be aware of the risk of losing clients.

2. Anxiety Management

The symptom of anxiety on the mental level is similar to the symptom of pain on the physical level. In the treatment process, especially in the face of trauma, events, and disturbing situations, anxiety may increase, which indicates the progress of the therapy technique and is usually transient. The psychotherapist should always be aware of and manage anxiety symptoms (Johari Fard, 2024).

3. Emotional Catharsis and Discharge

Another potential common feature that exists in most psychotherapy techniques is providing an opportunity for emotional catharsis. In most psychotherapy approaches, clients are allowed to talk about their problems in order to express their repressed emotions by expressing their life events and feelings about these problems. Providing an opportunity for the individual to release the psychological pressure caused by problems and the feelings arising from them sometimes has a therapeutic effect for some clients (Johari Fard, 2024).

4. Increasing Awareness

Although traditionally, increasing awareness and making clients more insightful was done in an analytical approach, further examination of psychotherapy approaches and techniques shows that providing information, feedback, and various trainings, even in behavioral and cognitive approaches, increases the client's insight and awareness towards themselves, the problem, and their life in general (Johari Fard, 2024).

5. Strengthening Self-Esteem and Self-Efficacy

Often, the confidence that people have in their internal capabilities allows them to solve their internal and interpersonal problems. Therefore, if the therapist helps to restore and strengthen the person's Self-Esteem and Self-Efficacy, the client himself can help the treatment progress by relying on this sense of competence (Johari Fard, 2024).

6. The Client's Imitation and Modeling of the Therapist

Often, when the therapist presents his technique or advice, the client pays close attention to his appearance and behavior to find out whether the therapist has applied such advice to himself. For example, when the therapist teaches the relaxation technique, the client monitors the therapist to see if he is in a relaxed state or if he is restless.

Of course, some clients, especially when the therapeutic relationship is strong, go to extremes and imitate the therapist's behaviors and speech. They even repeat his or her words. For this reason, novice therapists are advised to practice each technique on themselves many times before presenting it to clients. In this way, they will both help improve their own health and be a suitable role model for clients (Johari Fard, 2024).

7. Training and Strengthening Adaptive Responses

If we consider one of the indicators of mental health to be adaptation to external conditions, the goal of most psychotherapy techniques is to train and strengthen adaptive behaviors and skills and reduce maladaptive behaviors. Skills such as assertiveness, relaxation, problem solving, and self-working are among these (Johari Fard, 2024).

8. Suggestion (Induction)

Just as placebo is effective in the healing process of chemical drugs, this point is more evident in psychotherapy, where a stronger therapeutic relationship is established between the therapist and the client. After the end of a therapy session, the client feels better and more relaxed and even strengthens the expectation of solving his problems within himself, and this has nothing to do with the type of psychotherapy method or technique. Clinical experiences show that suggestion has a strong correlation with the therapeutic relationship (Johari Fard, 2024).

In addition to the above factors, many other researchers and authors of psychotherapy, such as Procheska, Norcross, Currie, etc., have brought other common or non-specific factors in psychotherapy systems, and here, we mention another example of these common factors:

In a study, Miller and Sanchez (1994) have identified the following six effective factors from examining various psychotherapy techniques:

1. Giving **Feedback** to clients,
2. Emphasis on personal **Responsibility;**
3. Direct Advice,
4. Providing a **Menu** of methods and techniques,
5. **Empathy,**
6. Strengthening **Self**-efficacy.

The term FRAMES is derived from the combination of the words "Feedback, Responsibility, Advice, Menu, Empathy, and Self-efficacy" mentioned in the above factors.

Chapter 2

Who is a psychotherapist?

Chapter 2
Who is a psychotherapist?

"Therapist as medicine" is a famous phrase in clinical medical and therapeutic interventions and means the importance of the therapist's position and personality in the therapeutic process. Therapy is not simply the presentation of several therapeutic techniques, but a communicative, semantic and dynamic context of the therapist's personality and the client. For this reason, regardless of any type of therapy, the therapist's personality and behavior have an impact on the therapeutic processes.

Therapist's Personality

The therapist's personality is a set of relatively stable internal characteristics that can positively or negatively affect the context therapy and the results of the treatment. Scientific literature in recent decades has shown that regardless of the therapeutic approach (cognitive, analytical, existential, behavioral, etc.), the therapist's personality characteristics play a decisive role in the quality of the treatment process.

According to the NEO five-factor model of personality, these five dimensions have a great influence on the therapist's work:

1. *Extraversion:* The ability to communicate effectively with clients, express oneself, and be socially interested.
2. *Agreeableness:* Traits such as empathy, kindness, and flexibility.
3. *Conscientiousness:* Conscientiousness and commitment, and maintaining professional boundaries.
4. *Neuroticism:* The ability to tolerate stress and remain calm in difficult sessions.
5. *Openness:* Acceptance of differences, creativity, and openness to different treatment methods.

Also, other studies have shown that the following factors are effective in the psychotherapy process:

1. *Self-awareness:* Awareness of personal history and personal biases.
2. *Reflective functioning:* The ability to analyze one's own and the client's emotions.
3. *Empathy:* The most important predictor of therapeutic alliance.
4. *Self-compassion:* increased resilience and reduced burnout (Norcross & Goldfried, 2005; Elliott et al., 2011; Grammer, 2013).

Common Factors in Psychotherapists

Research shows that beyond the different contents of psychotherapy, there are common factors among professional therapists that increase the effectiveness of therapeutic techniques. These factors include:

1. Listening: It can be said that one of the most important activities of a psychotherapist is listening. As a professional listener, a psychotherapist must know the skills of this work.[1]

Listening in psychotherapy is an active process and is linked to other activities of the psychotherapist. During active listening, the therapist evaluates the client's statements, observes his behavior, decides whether to ask the client now or to Hesitation his questions, offers recommendations, interpretations, and suggestions, and may even change the focus of the interaction. The therapist must also be careful about every point the client says about how the treatment is going or about himself, so that he can intervene when necessary. Therefore, listening is not a simple activity and requires training, skill development, and practice. The best practice is to review recorded sessions under the supervision and periodic supervision of a psychotherapist. With this method, you will realize the number of times you should have responded or remained silent, and you will understand when your words interrupted the client's flow of conversation about important topics, or when your statements and recommendations were not a real response to the client's statements (Johari Fard, 2024).

2. Reflection: Another type of psychotherapeutic response that person-centered therapists have studied and emphasized is reflection. This phenomenon is referred to as the therapist's ability to reflect the client's views in an empathetic atmosphere (Rogers, 2003) and is highly dependent on listening skills, because effective

---

1- For more information, read the book «Psychotherapy Techniques based on Approaches and Methods» by Reza Johari Fard.

and accurate reflection occurs when the therapist understands the client.

Reflection is a manifestation of empathic response or the therapist's ability to reflect the client's expressed feelings and establish a connection with him. Rogers (2003) emphasizes the importance of the therapist's empathic response in the treatment process by referring to the following formulation:

According to this formulation, the therapist's responsibility is to understand the world as she sees it, to the best of her ability and based on the client's "internal frame of reference" ... to set aside all perceptions arising from the "external frame of reference" when working with the client and to convey elements of empathetic understanding to the client.

The skill of reflection has sometimes been called "clinician sensitivity," and when used naturally and sincerely (rather than artificially and excessively), it can help facilitate the emergence of a therapeutic alliance, especially in the early sessions.

Reflective listening skills fall into four categories:

2.1. Explanation: It is a concise response to the speaker that conveys the essence of what the speaker meant in the listener's language.

2.2. Reflection of feelings: This is to return to the speaker's emotions and feelings in short sentences. To improve your reflection of feelings skills, you can use the following four skills:

2.2.1. Focus on emotional words;
2.2.2. Pay attention to the overall content of the message;
2.2.3. Observe body language;
2.2.4. Ask yourself how I would feel if I were experiencing such a situation.

2.3. Reflection of Meaning: When feelings and facts are combined in a short response, reflection of meaning is achieved. As Robert Karkoff said, it is easier to act on what we have in our minds than to act on what we only feel in our hearts. Our listening is most effective when we respond to the speaker's meaning and intent, the feelings that excite or provoke him, as well as the content that accompanies the feeling. When a person knows how to reflect feeling and content separately, it is easier to include both in the reflection of meaning. When learning the first reflection of meaning, it is useful to use the following formula:

"You feel..........., because...........", for example: You feel happy because your life is going well in every way.

2.4. Summarizing Reflection: Summarizing reflection is a brief and concise repetition of the main themes and feelings that the speaker has raised in a long section of conversation and, as a result, cannot be reflected by one of the previously mentioned skills. With the help of this skill, some of the recent conversations can be connected and feelings or issues can be expressed more clearly and vividly by retelling them briefly.

3. Problem-Solving Ability: Since each client usually enters the therapy room with a problem, the therapist's ability to identify the main problem and provide solutions to overcome that problem should be considered as one of the characteristics of professional psychotherapists (Johari Fard, 2024).

4. Suggestion: In addition to problem-solving ability and during therapy, the therapist gives suggestions to his clients. These suggestions have been of interest to directive behavior therapists in the past and are seen today in the form of homework in cognitive-behavioral psychotherapies, but psychoanalytic therapists and person-centered psychotherapists pay less attention to them.
Suggestions can be presented in a variety of ways. For example, some suggestions are expressed in a commanding and parental manner, similar to military orders. This approach not only reinforces the client's feelings of weakness and helplessness, but also, given the judgmental nature of the suggestion (which recommends good and bad, dos and don'ts, etc.), can be a weakness for a clinician who must maintain an impartial position.

Other suggestions are presented in a so-called Socratic style to enhance the individual's reflection. For example, "Why don't you try this?" instead of imperative sentences like "do this!", or "Do you think it would be a good idea to set up a schedule for your home activities?" In this way, while presenting the suggestion, the client is invited to reflect on and cooperate with the suggestion. This approach can be considered a type of adult-adult communication.

5. Explanation and Interpretation: Most therapists have observed confusion and behavioral, cognitive, and emotional irregularities in their initial encounters with clients, and perhaps for this reason, clients are very insistent on understanding the why and explanation of their problem. At this time, the therapist's explanation and interpretation skills can effectively and appropriately organize and clarify the client's mind.

Traditionally, explanation and interpretation skills were used in psychoanalytic and analytical approaches, which you can read in detail in the psychoanalysis chapter. This is important to note for several reasons: The client may have unrealistic expectations or expectations that are incompatible with the type of treatment chosen when entering the therapy session. Therefore, the therapist should inform the client of his or her role in the treatment and the importance of his or her cooperation and agreement.

6. Education: Typically, psychoeducational therapies such as cognitive-behavioral therapy involve providing information and educating clients. Education and information provision should be directed toward therapeutic goals and to clarify the path of treatment, and unnecessary and scattered information should be avoided. Also, if the therapist describes the client's problem in simple terms from a psychological perspective, this awareness will reduce the client's anxiety and actively strengthen his or her contribution and role in the treatment process. In fact, education should facilitate the treatment path; otherwise, providing information and education that diverts the client's focus from the main path is not recommended.

7. Confrontation: All therapeutic approaches believe that confronting oneself/the past/trauma/unconscious/anxious situation, etc., has greater therapeutic effects than avoiding/denying/suppressing/not expressing, etc. Psychotherapists must use this skill with sensitivity and intelligence. This requires establishing a therapeutic relationship with trust and confidence in the client. Otherwise, the client may consider the confrontation as a form of attack, become agitated, and even leave the therapy session. In other words, first a therapeutic relationship and a foundation for trust and psychological security must be established, and then the individual must be invited to the confrontation.

8. Reassurance: This skill, like other skills, requires the therapist to be alert when using it, otherwise it will usually have little effect. The therapist's reassurance statements should be relevant to the client's major issues and critical experiences in life. The important point is that the therapist should not use false and unfounded (especially scientifically) reassurances simply to please the client or those around him.

9. Self-disclosure: In most clinical situations, there are cases that are similar to the therapist's life situation. The question that arises here is whether psychotherapists are allowed to self-disclose and express their experiences and life secrets.

The answer to this question depends largely on the therapist's personality traits, the type of problem, and so on. However, some sources have emphasized therapist self-disclosure (e.g., Joward, 1971; Garfield, 1996).

Although the therapist's self-disclosure can be a sign of his interest in the client's life, there is also a risk that the therapist's personal experience may be useless and even dangerous for the client (given their personality differences) and that, in the client's view, it may be considered a form of excessive self-expression on the part of the therapist. Therefore, therapists must be careful and vigilant in using this technique, as with the other skills mentioned (Johari Fard, 2024).

10. Role Playing: Most therapists have experienced this point in dealing with different clients and in order to express or teach their clients, they have to role play some techniques or skills (such as social skills or self-expression) and sometimes, in family psychotherapy, how spouses deal with each other in a practical way. For this purpose, psychotherapists need to acquire role-playing skills and techniques.

11. Questioning: Therapists usually ask more questions in the first few sessions than in subsequent sessions. The general rule is that the therapist should ask questions of their clients if there is insufficient information on any topic. In the first sessions, it is best to start with open-ended and general questions and then narrow down the scope of the questions and ask them in a closed-ended manner.

In systemic approaches, the purpose of asking questions is not only to obtain information, but also to contribute to the creation of information. In other words, in these approaches, questioning itself is considered a type of therapeutic intervention, such as rotational questioning, differential questioning, etc.

11. Homework: The use of homework is one of the techniques emphasized by cognitive-behavioral approaches. However, today its usefulness is known in most psychotherapy approaches.

For example, if a person is suffering from some kind of anxiety and the therapist teaches him a relaxation technique, his real healing occurs when the person experiences this technique repeatedly and in the context of his daily life and generally in a real situation. Paying attention to this fact involves several points worth considering. First, the client will have an active and responsible role in the psychotherapy and healing process. Second, the client will find the place of that technique or skill in his daily life and will not consider this technique as a disturbing and additional factor in his life. Third, by reviewing these assignments in future sessions, the therapist can evaluate the recovery process.

Another noteworthy point in using this technique is that psychotherapists must provide the client with an assignment that is appropriate to the client's problem, personality, behavioral, cognitive characteristics, lifestyle, and abilities (Johari Fard, 2024).

Chapter 3

Self-Working

Systemic Thinking To Psychotherapy

Chapter 3

Self-Working: Systemic Thinking To Psychotherapy

Andreas Fitzer and Rainer Schwing, in their book "Systemic Counseling and Psychotherapy," believe that the future of psychotherapy lies in the combination of treatments, but not in a combination like "Goulash" (meat stew), but in an organized and conscious arrangement of approaches and methods like shish kebab!

The theoretical model of psychotherapy techniques based on approaches and methods is a way to consciously and systematically arrange treatments. However, in order for a therapist to be able to artistically put these approaches and methods together, I have introduced the model of the "System Thinking Psychotherapy Triangle" (Johri Fard, 2017; 2024). This model is composed of the following three dimensions:

1. Knowing Approaches

In these approaches, various types of analysis, dynamics, systems, and the like are used to better understand the etiology and understanding of the problem and symptoms of the disease. In these approaches, we want to examine the clinical treatment path both horizontally and vertically (in depth) so that the therapist does not consider the symptoms and disorders as a single factor, but rather takes a deeper look at them, and also, the client's awareness and perception matures session by session.

2. Doing Approaches

In these approaches, actions, tools, and therapeutic techniques are addressed. Techniques that are increasing in number every day and include hundreds of relaxation methods and techniques, hypnotherapy, behavioral techniques, cognitive, ACT, and the like. Today, a therapist who does not know these techniques is literally "behind the scenes" and, more clearly, far from the pragmatic community of therapists.

3. Being Approaches

In these approaches, the therapist is an empathetic listener and companion of the client, and the therapist's genuine "presence" and "being" in the therapy session are important. In Rogers' theory, the experience of presence means the therapist's "being here and now" in a "mind-conscious" way in the therapy session. Many existential and humanistic approaches have addressed the dimension of being.

The table below provides a summary of psychotherapy techniques based on approaches and methods and with a systems thinking perspective. The content of this table includes all the famous therapists of these approaches, but due to the large number of names, we have limited ourselves to a few familiar names.

Approaches Methods	Doing Approaches			Knowing Approaches		Being Approaches		
	First Generation in Behaviorism	Second Generation in Behaviorism	Third Generation in Behaviorism	Individual Analysis	System Analysis	Humanism	Existential Therapy/Reality Therapy	Transpersonal Therapy
Individual Methods	Skinner/Wolpe	Ellis/Beck	Kabat-Zinn/Hayes	Freud/Eric Berne/Malan	Selvini-Palazzoli/Chechnya	Rogers	Rollo May/Glasser	Assagioli/Rowan
Group Therapy	Behavioral/Cognitive/Act Groups			Analytical/Family Group Therapy		Encounter/Existential/Mean Therapy Groups		
Family Therapy	Pettson/Stewart/Lieberman			Ackerman/Frimou/Scharff/Nagi		Satir/Symbolic Family Therapy Whitaker		
Art Therapy	Cognitive-Behavioral Art Therapy			Art Therapy such as Painting/Analytical and Family Storytelling		Humanistic Art Therapy		
Play Therapy	Cognitive-Behavioral Play Therapy			Individual or Family Analysis with Play/Sand/Dolls/Family Board		Xline Child-Centered Play Therapy		
Mind-Body Methods	Cognitive Hypnotherapy/Relaxation			Hypnoanalysis		Transcendental Meditation/Yoga		

Table 3.1 Summary of Psychotherapy Techniques Based on Approaches and Methods And With a Systems Thinking Perspective (Johari Fard, 2024)

Self-working is a therapeutic training program that is based on the principles of system-based psychotherapy influenced by world-renowned approaches in psychology and psychotherapy, including psychoanalysis, exchange analysis, schema therapy, Rogers' person-centered therapy, acceptance and commitment therapy, and the like, but it has completely cultural, indigenous assumptions that arise from the Iranian lifestyle (Johari Fard, 2024; 2025).

The term self-working is made up of two parts: "self" and "working." Working here means "to work and practice". In fact, self-working is a type of work that has four characteristics: conscious, mature, responsible, and creative. So self-working involves working with the personality in a conscious, mature, responsible, and creative way. These four characteristics are discussed in detail in the third and final part of self-working, but it is considered by the therapist from the very first exercises. For example, when we say, "body-working", it means working with the body in a conscious, mature, responsible and creative way. And what is meant by "emotion-working" is working with emotion in a conscious, mature, responsible and creative way. Thus, this meaning resides in the word "working" as it appears throughout this book (Johari Fard, 2024; 2025).

Chapter Four

Theoretical Foundations of Self-Working

Chapter Four

Theoretical Foundations of Self-Working

Although self-working is a therapeutic educational program, every practical program must have strong theoretical foundations and assumptions, so that educational and therapeutic techniques can be formed correctly. In this chapter, we introduce the fundamental assumptions and theoretical principles of self-working.

Assumptions of Self-Working

The first assumption: Life is a path that starts from a source (past) and moves towards a destination (future).

This assumption is completely derived from Eastern and Iranian culture, which has its roots in our ancient literature and mysticism. In many works of the past, the path-oriented method and dynamism in the path of life can be seen:

A religion resembles a skin, a truth a brain
Between both, a path exists! (Shabestari, Persian Poet)

This assumption is consistent with existential theories, humanism, narrative therapy, and acceptance and commitment. In these approaches, past, present, and future are key dimensions of human experience which play a role in the reconstruction of personality and life.

The second assumption: A healthy (normal) person is aware of his life path and consciously steps along this path, accepting responsibility for his steps.

This assumption can be examined based on the theories of mindfulness, Acceptance and Commitment Therapy (ACT), and Dialectical Behavior Therapy (DBT). These approaches emphasize mindful living.

The third assumption: Mental health means living consciously, maturely, responsibly and creatively in life.

This assumption shows a comprehensive idea about human living with four autonomous actions and is related to many psychological and psychotherapy approaches such as Kohlberg's concepts of moral development, emotional maturity, Eric Berne's theory of Transactional Analysis, Klasser's choice theory, art therapy theories and the like.

The fourth Assumption: The abnormal person does not have a clear path in life and feels confused and futile in life.

This assumption is consistent with psychodynamic perspectives. In these theories, the unconscious is seen as a source of conflict, avoidance, and maladaptive behaviors. Freud, Jung, and others emphasized that personality development requires confronting the content of the unconscious and moving toward self-awareness. Research has shown that the unconscious can lead to impulsive decision-making, poor planning, and reduced emotional control. This assumption is also consistent with existential, semantic, and humanistic approaches.

The fifth Assumption: Recovery is a dynamic process, not a static and fixed goal; mental health is in its fluidity.

This assumption emphasizes the dynamics of mental growth and the process-oriented nature of mental health, and is in line with new psychological models such as positive psychology, acceptance and commitment therapy, and developmental psychology. Mental health, like physical health, requires continuous exercise throughout life, not at a specific time, and self-working is a kind of continuous exercise of the personality (Johari Fard, 2024).

The sixth Assumption: In self-working, the path of treatment focuses on rebuilding oneself and one's life path rather than treating the symptoms of harm.

This assumption is consistent with new directions such as positive psychology, empowerment-oriented therapies, and future-oriented models in psychotherapy (Johari Fard, 2014).

Self-Working Conceptualization

As mentioned in the assumptions of self-working, psychological harm from the perspective of self-working is the result of confusion in understanding one's life path. In my opinion, this confusion in the path of life begins with misperception of one's self-concept, real self, ideal self, strengths and weaknesses, capabilities, and even a lack of proper understanding of external conditions and opportunities, and lays the foundation for many subsequent incorrect decisions. In order for an individual to take a step on the path of mental health, three stages of self-working must be completed (Johari Fard, 2024; 2025):

1. Being-on-This: I have made this word from the three parts "on", "this" and "being". "On" refers to the conscious attitude of mindfulness and awareness (according to Heidegger, transcendental perception) of the individual on himself. “On” has a conscious, holistic, non-judgmental and dynamic view, in contrast, (in) being-in-itself, which is an autistic (remaining in oneself), willless and unconscious view of oneself.

“This” refers to what is here/now and the self, as it is, not as it should be. In fact, the reason for many of the unattainable and “unbecoming” is the lack of understanding and acceptance of the conditions of “this” and living in the illusions and fantasies of “that”, that which has not yet been achieved and is only in our minds. Therefore, on this being invites us to know ourselves as we are. The combination of “being present” means consciously recognizing and accepting one’s present circumstances.

2. Becoming-to-That: It refers to the direction of the person’s look and life path. It also refers to the ideals, values, and goals of the person in life, what must be created and moved towards. It should be stated that without creating them, a person is stuck in place, he is passive and as if confused. This stage of treatment is attractive to many people because they find the meaning of their life and understand which direction they are living in. Becoming emphasizes the gradual occurrence of change and shows the person’s desire, will, and adaptation. Therefore, it means creating that and having a desire towards it.

3. Life-Theme: The term “theme” is a legacy of my years working in the world of art, and especially music. Theme is a fundamental and very practical concept in art, and every artist begins to create a work from a mental idea that will eventually become the theme of his work. The fingerprint of the distinction of the works is in this theme, and the more artistically an artist creates a theme, his work will remain more in the memories and recollections.
In my opinion, life is the most important work of art, the artist of which is the individual himself, who must creatively create

a theme for it, and this creation does not occur except with two previous stages; first, " Being-on-This " (conscious recognition and acceptance of one's present conditions) and " Becoming-to-That " (the realistic creation of ideals and the direction of life), which will ultimately lead to the emergence of the "life-theme."

1- Being-on-This (Beginning) → **3-Life-Theme** → 2- Becoming-to-That (Destination)

1. Hierarchy of the stages of " Being-on-This

In the first stage (Being-on-This), which is like the psychoanalist working on the individual's past, the goal is to understand and analyze the individual's past, with the difference that I do this analysis in a systematic and step-by-step manner. This process works as follows:

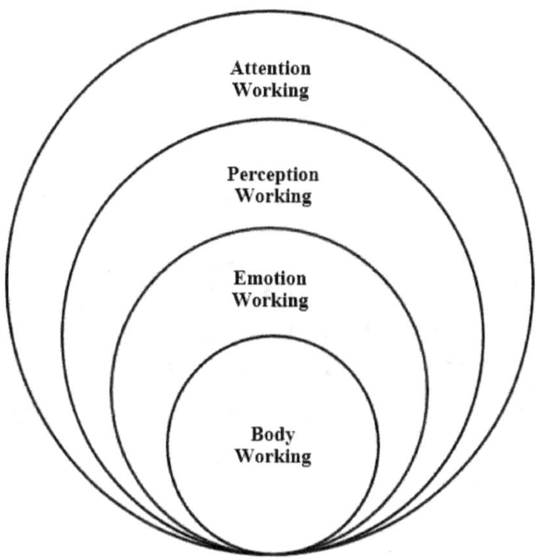

Figure 1. The hierarchy of the stages of " Being-on-This " (Johari Fard, 2024)

The order of this pattern, namely working on the body, emotion, and perception, is derived from the three-brain theory (Paul McLean, quoted by Gray, 2007), which states that the human skull does not contain just one brain, but rather contains three brains, each of which represents a gradual evolutionary interval of layers and cortexes that have formed on top of the older layer. He calls them the "triad" or "trinity" of the brain (Gray, 2007). Based on the three-brain theory and from an evolutionary perspective, the new layer of the brain, the neocortex, is similar to the limbic brain of modern mammals. The oldest is attributed to the brain of ancient mammals, and the third layer, the oldest, is attributed to the brain of reptiles. I have added a new level, attention, to this brain model, because attention is the highest and the only brain activity specific to humans, and by paying attention to and cultivating it, all previous levels can be maintained. This model is in line with the evolutionary theories of the brain, and in fact, growth, development, and evolution (Johari Fard, 2024; 2025).

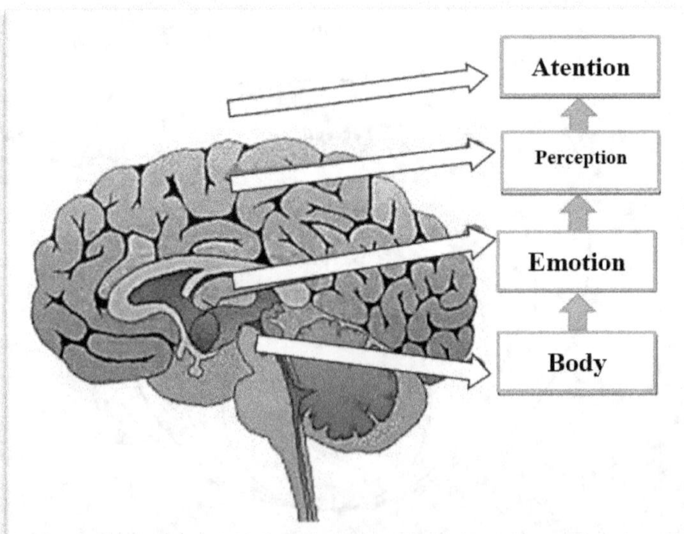

Figure 2. Neuropsychological model of self-control
(Four-level brain model, Johari Fard, 2024; 2025)

Theoretical Principles of Self-Working

The theory of "self-Working" as a new approach in psychotherapy aims to provide a comprehensive framework for psychological regeneration, inner growth, and individual meaning-seeking by combining the four levels of human lived experience (body, emotion, perception, and attention). To establish this theory on a scientific basis, its theoretical principles must be clearly explained. This section discusses the principles that formulate the existential philosophy and internal mechanism of self-efficacy based on an interdisciplinary integration of psychology, philosophy, neuroscience, and anthropology.

First Principle: Self-Working, Conscious Recreation of Mental Existence in the Context of Time

Self-working is a conscious, dynamic and multi-level process through which an individual can recreate his/her mental existence in the three dimensions of past (Being-on-This), present (Life-Theme) and future (Becoming-to-That) in a conscious, mature, responsible, and creative manner. This process, by utilizing the capacities of the body, emotion, perception and attention, leads to the individual's internal redesign.

Principle Two: Self-Working, a Psychological Response to Existential Ruptures

At the heart of human existence, challenges such as meaninglessness, death, loneliness, and responsibility confront the individual. Self-working acts as a psychological response to these fundamental ruptures; a response that goes through the path of rebuilding the human relationship with the self, the past, the future, and others, and illuminates the path of the individual's life.

Principle Three: Self- Working, a Redesign of Lived Experience

From a phenomenological perspective, self-working is the process of redesigning the conscious experience of a person. This redesign occurs at the physical, emotional, perceptual, attentional, and future levels. In this sense, self-working is an attempt to live with a new quality and create a new form of "being."

Principle Four: Self-Working, a Rewriting of the Inner Narrative

Every human being has an inner narrative about who and what he or she is. These narratives, often formed in childhood and influenced by traumatic experiences, can be limiting. Self-working rewrites these narratives by intervening in them so that the individual can live with a new, responsible, and creative story.

Principle Five: Self-Working, a Regulatory Cybernetic System

Self-working is a system that uses internal and external feedback to intelligently regulate the body, emotion, perception, attention, and the future. By correcting perceptual and behavioral errors, this system leads to more effective adaptation to the self, others, and the environment.

Principle Six: Self-Working, Trans-Evolutionary Awareness

One of the unique capacities of humans is the ability to "consciously reconstruct the self." Self-discipline is a manifestation of this trans-evolutionary capacity. This process allows the individual to not only let go of the past, but also to create a future consistent with their values and ideals.

Seventh Principle: Self-Working, a Context-Based Theory

In psychotherapy, some approaches, such as psychoanalysis and cognitive behavioral therapy, emphasize content, and some, such as ACT theories or systemic theories, emphasize context. Self-working is an approach that focuses on both content and context and intertwines both; techniques and concepts derived from Eastern cultural contexts and western scientific psychology (Johari Fard, 2024).

The Place of Self-Working in Psychotherapy

"Self-Working" is a systems thinking approach that, by integrating theories from psychology, neuroscience, cognitive and dynamic psychotherapy, and philosophy of life, suggests a path that not only leads to symptom reduction, but also to acceptance and creation of oneself and life. Examining the differences between self-working and other therapies helps to better understand its place in the map of contemporary psychotherapy. Some of the fundamental differences between self-working and other therapies are:

1. Theoretical Origins

Many classical therapeutic approaches have originated from a main theoretical origin. For example, CBT therapy emphasizes cognitive-behavioral learning and psychoanalysis emphasizes working with the unconscious. While self-working is a systems thinking therapeutic approach and is influenced by various psychological approaches.

2. Time Span

Most therapeutic approaches emphasize a specific time, for example, psychoanalysis focuses on the past, and act focuses on the present. However, self-working covers three temporal dimensions: on the Being-on-This (working on the past); Becoming-to-That (future-practice); and on the Life-Theme (working on the present).

3. Unit of Intervention

In many therapies, the mind or behavior is considered the main unit of intervention. Self-working, however, activates the body, emotion, perception, and attention in a level-by-level manner and establishes interaction between these levels.

4. Dynamic Process of Treatment

In conventional therapies, the path is linear from problem to analysis and then to change. However, in self-working; in a cyclical and reversible manner, each stage can reinforce the previous or subsequent stages (self-working cycle).

5. Levels of Intervention

Classical approaches usually work on one or two levels (e.g., cognition and behavior). Self-working links four main levels with two complementary dimensions (future working and life working).

Strengths of Self-Working

1. *Multi-level* integration: simultaneous work with the body, emotion, perception, and attention.
2. *Three-dimensionality in time*: working on the past, present, and future.
3. *Cyclical structure:* return and repetition in order to consolidate change.
4. *Focus on self-creation:* beyond problem solving, creating the self, life, and future.
5. *Cultural localization capability:* flexibility in adapting to the cultural context.
6. *Intrapersonal and interpersonal continuity:* impacting social relationships and roles and the balance between self-working and otherness.
7. *Application beyond clinical treatment:* suitable for training, coaching, and personal development (Johari Fard, 2025).

Chapter Five

The Seven Responses to Psychological Challenges
(Self-Working Perspectives)

Chapter Five

The Seven Responses to Psychological Challenges (Sel-Working Perspectives)

Self-working perspectives examines analyses and opinions related to self-working in seven responses in order to reflect on some psychological challenges. These perspectives help therapists and clients better understand the concepts of self-working.

First Challenge: In the Deception of Perception

Life begins from the first days of birth, but it will take years for each person to understand the concept of life. The concept of life is a very personal and phenomenological concept that everyone understands in their life world and phenomenal world and is related to many variables inside and outside the person. But the greatest role in this is played by the person's perception, which is the process of giving meaning to phenomena.

Perception creates concepts for us, and these concepts connect the external and strange world with our internal and personal world, and consequently, such a process, like a double-edged sword, can be both practical and useful for the person and ineffective and harmful. Because, the formation of a wrong concept will lead to a wrong understanding of many phenomena, and of course, such damage will be greater for abstract concepts such as freedom, progress, success, love, and the like. For example, if a person has a wrong understanding of the concept of success since childhood, then he wants to be successful at all costs and may cause a lot of harm to himself and those around him in this way. I consider the first hesitation of self-working to be "in the illusion of perception" and I think it is better to become more familiar with the illusions of this psychological phenomenon.

Jean Lacan, a famous French psychoanalyst, believes that the human psyche is composed of three parts (matter, aspect): Imagination, Symbolic, and Reality. In this triangle, the imaginary (I) refers to the endless search for discovery and knowledge. Knowledge that begins in childhood and others (people and objects) act as a mirror to help the child gain a complete picture of himself, the child first differentiates between self and other and conceptualizes the world for himself, and as mentioned, the child first understands the concepts of father, mother, affection, freedom, love, hatred, grudge, family, friend, and thousands of other concepts, and the volume of these concepts further expands the scope and world of his imagination.

Lacan believes that in the modern era, the imaginary and the individual's preoccupation with himself and the fantasy of conquering the world reach their peak, and this is a painful reality for the modern generation! For a generation that spends all its efforts in a "perfectionist" and endless way to "obtain", whether this acquisition is objective or abstract, material or immaterial, the important thing is to satisfy this endless desire and desire to obtain. The source of these desires must be found in this imaginary world and the aspect of human imagery that imagination takes shape and energy is spent on obtaining it, but unfortunately, this imagination can be fleeting and exciting,

and at any moment, the individual is caught up in another imagination. The aspect of human imagination is the origin of all progress and art, so long as imagination is not involved, "something" will not appear in the real world and life without imagination will be very boring.
The illusion of perception at this level is related to the mirror stage, when the child sees his or her own image in a mirror and first encounters the "self" as an imaginary whole. The ego is constructed here on the basis of "representation" and "imagination," not reality. In this order, our perception is based on "analogies," "adaptations," and "projections." We see the world more as we want or fear it to be, rather than as it is.

Interpersonal relationships (especially romantic or competitive relationships) are full of perceptual illusions that arise from unconscious fantasies and myths. For example, a person may perceive their boss as a threat because they have unconsciously replaced him or her with their powerful father. Therefore, the goal of self-working is to recognize the capabilities of this aspect of humanity, and to answer this important question: why are some people able to turn their fantasies into reality while others are unable to implement them?

The second facet of Lacan's triangle deals with the Real (R), a realm that refers to life and the world of existence. The world and phenomena that, until they are "known" and then "named," are incomprehensible and meaningless. Such as some mental illnesses, the unknowns of physics, or diseases like AIDS or Corona.

The definition of reality in philosophy is very broad, of course, in the process of self-working, there is no need to enter into the philosophical discussions of realism. But in general, reality can be attributed to objective matters and events that everyone is aware of. Therefore, reality is a term in contrast to subjectivity and imagination. For example, sunrise as an objective and observable thing that everyone agrees on its presence can be considered a real thing (R). However, the way an individual perceives and imagines a sunny day, which is a personal, specific matter and depends on personality characteristics, is an imaginary thing (I).

Reality testing is one of the indicators of mental health, which is disrupted in psychotic individuals and the boundary between reality and fantasy is lost, and in neurotic individuals it functions relatively; and of course this relative reality testing is more damaging. Self-working is an approach to strengthening reality testing and distinguishing reality from fantasy; recognizing reality as it is, not as we think it should be.

The illusion of perception at this level is that we think we can understand or control everything, when there is always something "unintelligible" and outside the box.

The third facet of Lacan's triangle is the symbolic (S), which refers to concepts, signs, symbols, language, culture, and even law and social structures. Humans are trapped within the symbolic even before they are born, because they belong to a content context; to an ethnic group, language, culture, family, religion. Sometimes even before birth, a "name" is chosen for the child and certain "qualities" are attributed to the unborn child! In this way, it is as if we are condemned to perceive the world and external realities through the lens of "language" and to understand every "thing" in terms of perceived concepts!

Deception at this level is rooted in structured meanings that exist outside the individual and in the ''big Other.'' Language binds us to frameworks in which we unconsciously find subjectivation. For example, a person who perceives themselves as ''failed'' may be a victim of their father's language or culture, which defined success only in terms of wealth or power.

In other words, Lacan's triangle is the relationship between the world of reality and the mental and inner world, the symbolic (language, concepts, culture, etc.), and if such an assumption is correct, the limitations of the mind's connection with life become clear. The mental world can be likened to a "room" that has limited windows to the outside world. I have chosen this analogy of the room of the mind from the famous film "Room."

The connection of this "mind room" with the outside world is through the five senses (sight, hearing, touch, taste, smell), and if we also consider the limitations of the senses, then we will realize the limitations of perception.
Perception is the process of giving meaning and conceptualizing external phenomena and stimuli. However, perception can only understand "something" correctly when the "senses" transmit it well. Therefore, if a person has a weakness in one of the senses (for example, vision) and perceives something incorrectly (for example, seeing Hassan as Huossein), perception goes wrong and suffers from a so-called "illusion" or perceptual error.

Now imagine how the "mind room", with all these colorful and enchanting fantasies, and with this perceptual limitation, can deceive us and lead us to a path that we may never have a desire for.

I remember a young man, one of my clients, working for an oil and gas company in the south of the country and earning a relatively good income. In a meeting, he told me that he wanted to quit his job and open a music studio in Tehran and start producing music and artistic activities there. When I got to know his life and personality, I felt that this decision was one of those imaginary examples that had little connection with reality. I tried to explain the situation to him, but unfortunately, a few months later, he did what he wanted and returned to me with bankruptcy, loss of corporate job, and depression.

There are many people like this and they usually do not want to consult and ask for the opinion of others, because they consider what they have learned from reality to be enough for their imaginary decision.
Here, one should not be fooled by the famous saying, "To want is to be able." To want is a sacred thing and the beginning of every movement and movement in life. But to be able to do so, one must plan consciously, maturely, and of course responsibly.

Cognitive psychology researchers believe that the ''gate'' through which we perceive the realities of the external world is called a ''schema.'' A schema is a mental framework for organizing information that allows us to make sense of external information in a short amount of time and make quick decisions and appropriate reactions using rules of thumb (heuristics). Sometimes this happens automatically and unconsciously, as a result of previous conditioning and learning (in the form of behavioral and cognitive habits). Schemas, which are formed from childhood and through the child's temperament, emotional needs, and parenting style, can distort our perception of reality in an adaptive or maladaptive way, and in a sense, the world is represented through the narrative of schemas.

For this reason, in the self-cultivation approach, before any change, we must look within ourselves beyond the perceptual allurements, the symbolic, and the world of concepts to find our "authentic" and real self, and by understanding our true talents and nurturing, growing, and developing them, we can rebuild our lives; but this time, with our own narrative, consciously and maturely in the path of our own life (Johari Fard, 2024).

Second Challenge: On Personality Changeability

There is a major challenge in psychology; is personality influenced by heredity or nurture? Does personality change? What is the right age to change? Is it not too late for a middle-aged person to change and alter personality? And...

Heredity or nurture each has its own proponents (see the personality theories of Schultz and Schultz), but I have a different answer to this challenge.

Undoubtedly, the first years of life are influenced by heredity and the maturation process. A process in which everything is planned in advance and according to this plan, the child's behaviors are formed and developed according to a specific schedule, and along with that, the parenting behaviors and the individual's environment lead to the formation of the first personality schemas. Such a formula is effective as long as we are "bound" by these schemas and "previous determinants", but, from the moment the individual's "consciousness" emerges and is on the path of "knowing" and "building", personality change begins, and if we take steps to understand our original personality and cultivate and direct it in the path of life, it is as if we have been born again.

Self-working is an approach that deeply believes in personality change based on increasing consciousness and expanding the individual's perception and awareness.

Third Challenge: Self-Knowledge or Self-Working

At first glance, you may find self-working a strange and unfamiliar word. However, I have used this word in contrast to self-knowledge or self-analysis. My main reasons for using "self-working" instead of self-knowledge are:

1. Self-working is a dynamic process that can continue throughout life, while self-knowledge or self-analysis considers the ''self'' as a static ''thing'' (object) that must be recognized at a fixed time and under fixed conditions. The dynamism inherent in the word self-working creates the ability in therapy to not neglect the ''self'' throughout life.

2. In self-working, dynamism and mobility in personality are considered, which requires a belief in free ''will'' and the process of personality growth and development in humans. Therefore, the self-working treatment method is based on freeing humans from the shackles of the past, incorrect upbringing, incompatible schemas, and everything that prevents a person from growth, development, and dynamism.

3. Self-working is composed of two parts, ''self'' and the verb ''to work,'' which means effort, continuous effort, and action. Therefore, self-working means continuous work and effort on one's personality, and just as we work on our body in sports, in self-working we work on our psyche and personality. So if we consider self-working as a continuous "work" and "effort" on one's personality, we must involve ourselves more in treatment and take more responsibility for growth and development in life.

Fourth Challenge: Self-Working: A System Thinking Approach to Psychotherapy

Today, we are witnessing many efforts in various scientific fields (especially the health system) to integrate and take a systems thinking view of important psychological achievements. Very important achievements in all three waves of psychology (psychoanalysis, behaviorism, and humanism) each opened new doors to the unknown and amazing realm of the human personality and psyche. However, the weakness of most of them was a one-dimensional and biased view of their findings. In a way, many students, specialists, and even the general public have been faced with the confusion of choosing and trying to find the best approach and treatment method.

Fortunately, with the acceptance of a holistic and systems thinking view and the possibility of "dialogue" between different psychological approaches and methods, the ground has been prepared for the design and emergence of more comprehensive and holistic treatments such as the self-working approach.

For this reason, the self-working approach is system-oriented, health-oriented, and based on human capabilities (resource-oriented) for growth and development in life. To achieve this goal, psychological and psychotherapy findings based on the Iranian-Islamic cultural context have been taken into account.

Fifth Challenge: Life Theme

One of the most common reasons people turn to a psychologist is confusion and uncertainty in life. The person does not know which path, work or goal is most suitable for their life. So, some of my clients in middle age seek to discover their hidden talents through trial and error, read different books, participate in different classes, and try out different jobs in their program, in order to find their peace.

Sixth Challenge: The Rhythm of Personality Development

If we imagine growth as a music that has a rhythm and beat, then this beat must occur at least between two beats, beat one...beat two...; like the rhythm of day...night...; black...white...; woman... man...; each of which can be associated with a two-beat song.

Now, to discover the rhythm of personality development and evolution, we must go to some psychological theorists who believe in development and evolution, such as Carl Rogers. According to Rogers, "self" as the most important part of personality is in two forms: "real self" and "ideal self". Real self refers to what "we are" and "were" our lives, and ideal self refers to what "we want" to be and "we look like" our lives. If the distance between the two is too great, the individual becomes ''self-incongruent" and discordant, and the rhythm of personality development does not proceed properly, and by ''denying" and ''distorting" realities, he tries to perceive himself or life in an unrealistic way. Such a person is undoubtedly not on the path of his life and is not satisfied with his life.

Therefore, it can be concluded that the rhythm of personality development, like other rhythms of nature that are double-beat, has two beats; the beat of ''this" and the beat of "that". The beat of this refers to the perception and awareness of what we are (being-on-this) and the beat of that refers to creation and the hope of achieving ideals and goals (becoming-to-that). By playing on the beats of this and that, the rhythm of development inspires personality and life to dance, dynamism, and flourishing, and frees us from isolation and stagnation (life-theme).

Seventh Challenge: Self-Working in Life

Self-Working, rather than being a psychological and academic theory, is a pragmatic and empirical approach to the transformation and growth of personality in the course of life, and therefore, true self-working occurs in the context of life, not in the therapy room.

For this reason, a workbook with exercises and case reports has been designed in Self-working that allows clients to experience each therapeutic educational topic in a practical way in the context of their own lives. In fact, self-working is for oneself and for life.

Self-working in everyday life means living consciously, responsibly, creatively and maturely. This educational and therapeutic path can show the following effects in a person's life:

• In Individual Life

Building an independent and autonomous personality: The person is responsible for his or her emotions, thoughts and behavior.

Moving from the role of victim to the role of activist: Rooting out past traumas, and breaking away from them.

Creating the future: With future-oriented exercises (such as discovering the ideal self; discovering strengths; discovering values).

• **In Interpersonal Relationships**

Leaving harmful re-creation patterns (for example, repetitive choices in love)

Discovering and repairing relationship root causes (for example: "need for approval" or "fear of abandonment")

Living with a mature and responsible theme.

• **In Work and Goal Setting**

Recognizing the inner meaning of work (not just income or prestige)

Focusing on creativity and value creation, living with a creative theme and not just quantitative success.

Choosing a career path based on discovering inner strengths

• **In Relation to Life and Existence**

Sense of ontological responsibility: living with a responsible theme

Creative meaning-making from suffering

Integration and harmony between being (being-on-this) and becoming (becoming-to-that).

Chapter Six

Theoretical and Clinical Foundations of Body-Working

Chapter Six

Theoretical and Clinical Foundations of Body-Working

The first step of self-working in the stage of "being-on-this", and based on the four-level model of the brain, is Body-Working or working with the body. The body can be the first support and guide to starting changes in oneself and life. If a change is going to occur in life, it is better to feel it in the body first, so that it can serve as a support for the next parts of the changes and also to feel good about ourselves. In this regard, many scientific sources prove that the body can be the first stage of working with the human psyche.

In the historical background of mind-body approaches, we can mention Raja Yoga exercises, which teach personality growth and transformation in eight stages. The first stages of work in this method are called Asana Yoga, which begins with physical exercises. From a physical perspective, Asanas are tools for achieving balance, strength, flexibility, agility and improving mental health, each of which in this sport is named with a specific name based on their execution nature, shape and overall structure (see http://yogini.ir/asana).

In the book “Theme Therapy”, I divided the human development process from childhood based on the “theme of life” into three periods: the physical life theme, the emotional life theme, and the cognitive life theme, which actually shows that every person starts life from the physical period and all the attention of those around a newborn in the first days of life is focused on his body and physiology, and will gradually follow his emotional and cognitive reactions.

Review of Body Working Techniques

Body-Working means working consciously, maturely, responsibly, and creatively with the body, and includes three parts: body awareness, body relaxation, and body training (Johari Fard, 2025). In the following, we will examine the theoretical foundations of these parts:

1. Body Awareness

Definition: The ability of a person to pay conscious attention to the body in order to be aware of the body and its behaviors. Techniques such as:

1.1 Body scan mindfulness: awareness of the body and physical behaviors.

1.2 Monitoring and recording daily body sensations (Body Awareness): The patient records his body sensations and links them to daily events.

1.3 Sensory grounding exercises or sense of awareness: Conscious attention to the five senses to be more aware of the body and its functions.

2. Body Relaxation

Definition: Reducing physical muscle tension and restoring a stable physiological state through relaxation techniques. It includes:

2.1 Progressive Muscle Relaxation (PMR): Regular contraction and release of various muscles in the body.

2.2 Diaphragmatic Breathing: or conscious breathing.

2.3 Massage and muscle relaxation techniques.

3. Body Learning

Definition: Learning new skills related to the body, including how to sit, walk, sleep, study, and other healthy behaviors and movements, regulating energy, and using the body creatively. Techniques include:

3.1 Alexander Technique: For body adjustment and conditioning, the effectiveness of Alexander Technique in reducing pain and psychosomatic disorders.

3.2 Training in self-expression (non-verbal techniques) such as mature standing, walking, voice formation and tone regulation, etc., and in general, body form correction in interpersonal communication.

3.3 Yoga, Pilates, and body corrective movements.

The following are two clinical examples of the application of body awareness and body exercise techniques in clinical work:

Closed Body - Open Body

A 35-year-old woman with a history of mood and anxiety disorders in her first sessions of self-working and body awareness practice drew her body state in a forward-facing manner. I called this state "closed body" in which the body and mind are in a closed, suppressed, and unspoken state (Body-Mind closed), and self-disclosure in the later stages will not be carried out properly until body-working and the change from a closed body to an open body occur (Johari Fard, 2024; 2025).

Case 2: Body in a Cage

A 33-year-old woman diagnosed with obsessive-compulsive disorder and panic disorder presented her body of awareness in a direct manner during the first sessions of self-working. In this exercise, the client suddenly felt a snake wrapped around her legs. This snake was not an illusion, but the return of a physical memory: an association with a silent fear from childhood. In self-working, these moments are the beginning of openness, the beginning of a path from a closed body to an open body and help in finding a foundation in the later stages (Johari Fard, 2024; 2025).

Chapter 7

Theoretical and Clinical Foundations of Emotion-Working

Chapter 7

Theoretical and Clinical Foundations of Emotion-Working

The second step of self-working in the stage of “being-on-this”, and based on the four-level model of the brain, is emotion-working or working with emotions. Emotions are an important part of states that have various effects on different dimensions of our academic, social, behavioral, motivational, mental health, and psychological well-being (Priese et al., 2020). The position and importance of working with emotions is mentioned in many psychological theories. Some of them are as follows:

Physiological perspective: According to the James-Lange theory and subsequent theories, emotions are physical-neural reactions whose perception shapes the emotional experience.

Psychoanalytic perspective: Suppressed emotions can be a source of internal conflict and psychological symptoms.

Cognitive perspective: Lazarus theory says that cognitive appraisal determines the intensity and quality of emotion.

Neurological perspective: The role of the amygdala in emotional processing, the prefrontal cortex in emotion regulation, and the connection of brain networks in inhibiting or facilitating the expression of emotion.

Evolutionary perspective: Emotions are adaptive systems that facilitate survival, social communication, and decision-making.

Theoretical and Neurological Foundations of Emotion in Self-Working

Our various emotions are processed in the limbic system, especially the amygdala. The various functions of the amygdala include:

1. It is unconscious in nature and operates without our awareness.
2. Past emotional memories are long-lasting and persistent, they are with us throughout life and can be activated in stressful situations.
3. They are activated automatically and without cognitive processing.
4. They act very quickly. In situations of danger, our emotional system acts faster than the cognitive system.
5. It has a general pattern of response and does not have precise knowledge of differences.

Therefore, the amygdala is involved in both emotional memory and emotional processing. The role of the amygdala in the memory system is to help the memory system retrieve information that is associated with different emotions. In other words, the amygdala stores and retrieves memories that have an emotional component. Another important role of the amygdala in the brain is in the creation and perception of emotional reactions. In other words, when we show different emotional reactions (such as fear, surprise, disgust, or joy) in response to a stimulus, the amygdala is active and, with the help of the cerebral cortex, allows us to perceive emotions. The role of the amygdala in the perception and recognition of emotions has been studied extensively. Based on the results of laboratory studies conducted on animals, it has been found that when the amygdala is stimulated with the help of small electrodes, the animal under test shows signs of different emotional states. The results of the above experiments

have also shown that when parts of the amygdala area of the brain of laboratory animals undergoing testing are destroyed, these animals are unable to show different emotional states and they cannot show emotions such as anger or fear in response to stimuli that normally stimulate these emotions.
The results of some studies show that when some psychological disorders (such as depressive disorder or obsessive-compulsive disorder) occur, changes occur in the functioning of the amygdala. Neuropsychologists believe that changes in the functioning of the amygdala are the main cause of the symptoms of depressive and obsessive-compulsive disorders.

When suffering from a depressive disorder, the activity of the amygdala increases. Also, the results of some studies show that the volume of the amygdala in patients with chronic depressive disorder has decreased. The results of research conducted on the function of the amygdala of the brain in patients with depressive disorder have shown that in these patients, the rate of recalling unpleasant memories has increased due to increased activity in the amygdala of the brain. These patients also recall words that have a threatening connotation to a greater extent in word retrieval tests. According to cognitive neuroscience researchers, increased activity in the amygdala of the brain is associated with a decrease in the release of the neurotransmitter serotonin, and a decrease in the release of the neurotransmitter serotonin is associated with the appearance of symptoms of disorders such as depressive disorder and obsessive-compulsive disorder.

Review and Analysis of Emotion-Working Techniques
Emotion-working, or more conscious, mature, responsible, and creative work with emotion, has three technical parts:

1. Release techniques
2. Externalization techniques
3. Core construct techniques (Johari Fard, 2024; 2025).

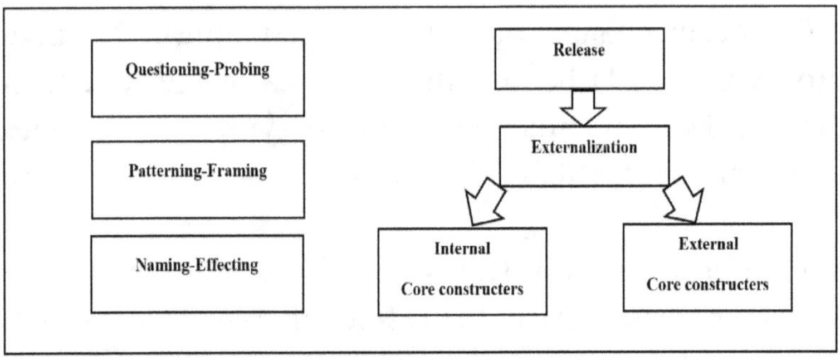

Figure 7.1 Stages and Techniques of Emotion-Working (Johari Fard, 2024; 2025).

Release

Release is a set of techniques that release psychic energy, repressed emotions, unspoken words, and other similar psychic material. However, there is no a specific goal or result. In fact, the goal of release exercises is to teach clients to release themselves and their inner energies. In other words, when a person is unable to release their repressed emotions and words, and sits silently and tightly in a therapy session, it is impossible to penetrate their emotional underlayers, problems, and traumas. This exercise is very useful for people who are closed-minded and have strict self-control, and reduces their resistance to therapy. For example, releasing the voice, releasing the feeling. However, for many people who have spent their entire lives suppressing their feelings and words, this is not an easy task. Release reduces resistance and gives the person a sense of liberation and peace due to the lack of focus on the specific goal and result of therapy, and working solely on releasing energies.

Externalization

Externalization, like release, deals with the discharge of psychic energies, emotions, and unspoken words. However, there is a difference here: we work purposefully and based on a specific object. For example, with the method of speaking or writing in the form of externalization, unspoken words and repressed feelings of childhood and adolescence are worked on specifically for the mother, and whenever the exercises for the mother object are finished, we turn to another object such as the father or grandmother, uncle, teacher, etc.

One of the common methods in psychoanalysis is to interpret through expressing the patient's associations, memories, and even dreams. While in self-working, one must wait until the person achieves emotional conditioning and emotional release, and gradually, with the help of the techniques of discovering the structure, we proceed from externalizations to discovering the structure.

York Becker believes that having no memories of childhood is like being condemned to drag a suitcase around with you without knowing what's inside, and as your life goes on, the suitcase gets heavier and you become more restless until you finally open it. The book Self-working provides exercises for externalization. For example, the exercise of rereading the past.

Core construct

Traditionally, many analytical therapies from the past to the present have worked on the emotions and traumas of the individual, and today, therapies such as schema therapy or emotion-focused therapy also have a special focus on emotion.

The difference between the self-working method in the emotional part and analytical approaches is that we first allow the patient to connect with their emotional part (for example, with release exercises) and then, externalizations are done solely in an emotional way. We avoid premature interpretation of becoming so that the individual gradually enters the perception stage by recognizing their own psychological frameworks (core construct) and learns how to analyze and process their past memories in a mature way on their own, and of course sometimes with the help of a therapist. Also, the difference between self-working in the emotion section and schema therapy is that, in schema therapy, the necessary psychological capacity for practicing with emotions is not created, while in self-working, the individual's psychological capacity is first developed in the conditioning stage, in order to prepare for working with their traumas and repressed emotions.

Core construct techniques are used by the therapist to discover external and internal core makers, including the following techniques:

A. Questioning-Probing (QP techniques)
B. Patterning-Framing (PF techniques)
C. Naming-Effecting (NE techniques)
(Johari Fard, 2024; 2025).

1. Questioning- Probing

Questioning-Probing techniques are used in self-working to discover the core construct and by the therapist, so that the patient, while talking and rereading the memories and unspoken things of his past, gradually moves towards working consciously, maturely, responsibly, and creatively with his past, and also prepares the groundwork for perception in the next stage (moving from the level of emotion to the level of perception).

Questioning-Probing techniques can be done in an intertwined manner, meaning that the therapist asks a question for the patient to reflect further in a Socratic way and at the same time guides the person towards further exploration of the roots and structures of his personality. In fact, a combination of cognitive and analytical techniques occurs. In questioning, the therapist should ask the patient to focus more on the areas in which he has problems and confront him with important issues of his personality and life, and not allow him to evade and enter into marginal discussions. Also, asking the patient to provide specific details and examples from life can be very helpful.

Patient: I was a loner and didn't interact much with my friends my age and those around me.
Therapist: Please explain in a little more detail.
Patient: My only connection to society was my uncle... He was the first person who noticed me and would take me to the alley and neighborhood to play with others. I was interested in soccer, but I didn't know how to play. When my uncle saw this passion and enthusiasm in me, he fostered it in me...
Therapist: So, didn't someone else see this interest? For example, my father or mother?
(This way of questioning led the patient to explore a number of topics and he answered after some reflection).
Patient: Yes, that's right... My father wasn't attentive... He didn't pay attention to me...
Therapist: Can you explain more? What kind of personality did your father have? And what kind of relationship did you have?
Patient: My father was an educated person, but he was very busy solving other people's problems and had almost no time for us... Not for me, not even my mother...

Techniques of Questioning-Probing

This section introduces some useful and practical questioning-probing techniques for therapists as examples and guidance. Examples of questioning techniques:

Roots Tree Technique

Starting with a current event or emotion, then asking ''What is behind this?" or ''Where is the root of this issue? Where does it lead?" We go back several layers to explore the foundations.

Event Chain Technique

Continuous questions ''What is important to you about this issue?" or ''How did you react like this?" until the answers reach a fundamental and foundational experience. Examples of exploring are as follows:

When this emotion forms in you, what memory or image comes to mind first?
When was the first time you had this feeling? In what circumstances?
What belief or thought is hidden behind this emotion?
If this emotion had a message, what would it say?
Who or what has played the most role in shaping this reaction in the past?
Have you seen a similar pattern in your family, school, or previous relationships?
If you were to describe this situation in a story, what would be your role in it?
What things would intensify or weaken this feeling?
If you were to explain this emotion to a child, how would you say it?
What parts of yourself do you not want to let go of this emotion, and why?

2. Patterning-Framing

Asmentioned, in self-working, after the release and externalization exercises, we reach the core construct stage. A stage in which the roots of personality formation are examined.

The best technique to patterning-framing is, to put together the memories, associations, dreams, and pure experiences of the individual's past to examine similarities, recurring patterns, and common denominators, and arrive at a pattern. I called this technique, core constructer network (sun network metaphor):

In self-working sessions with a woman in her 30s, with the help of questioning-probing techniques as well as patterning-framing techniques, we came to the following patterns:

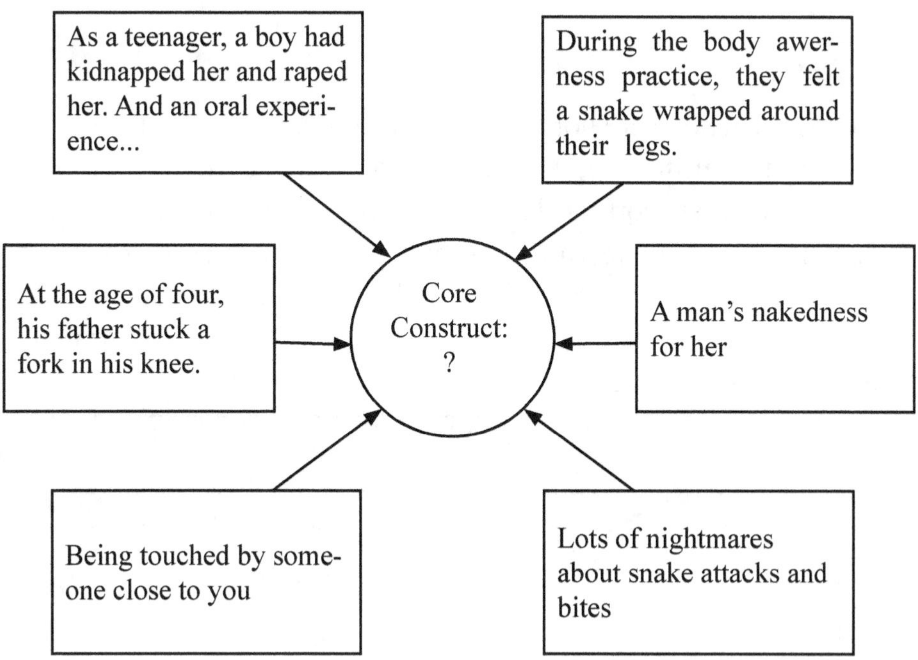

Fig. 7.2. core construct Network (sun network metaphor) (Johari Fard, 2025).

3. Naming-Effecting

After discovering the patterns and constructs, a name can be chosen for this construct with the cooperation of the client. The difference between this method and schema therapy is that, in schema therapy, the names and characteristics of the schemas are already specified and the therapist and the patient try to relate the individual's problem to one of the schemas (an example of the Procrustes bed error). This is similar to trying on a set of pre-made clothes to find the right size, but in self-working, the clothes are sewn for you.

Naming

In the example of Fig. 7.2. after considering these matters, client was asked to choose a name for his pattern. After reflecting and reviewing the evidence, she chose the name "Male Bite" for his model.

Effecting

Current reactions are not always "a response to this moment", but are strongly influenced by past experiences and core makers. At this stage, first work is done on external core constructers, that is, important people (objects), and in the manner of dynamic therapists, including David Malan, the Triangle of Person is used with slight modifications in the following way. We call this triangle the Triangle of Reactions:

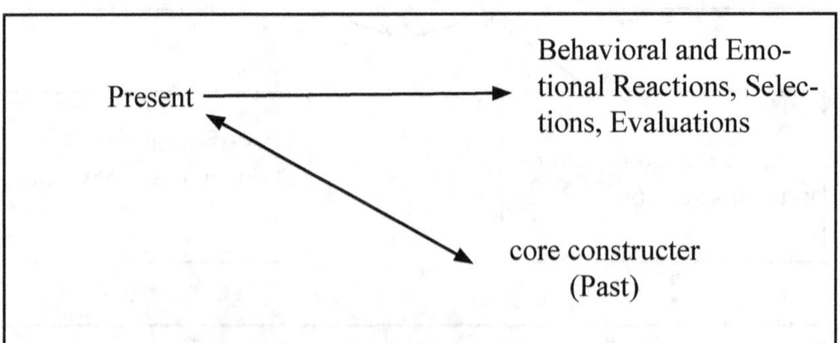

Figure 7.3 Triangle of Effeccting
(Johari Fard, 2024; 2025).

Working on the triangle of Effecting, along with ongoing externalization and release exercises, reveals external core constructers and many of the person's compulsive repetitive patterns, in the form of behavioral and emotional reactions, are discovered. The diagonal path from present to past is the activation of emotional memory or past structuralization in the present moment. By identifying this path, the therapist can discover early maladaptive patterns. This model helps the patient realize that many of his emotional-behavioral reactions stem from the past, not just current conditions (Represent).

Client: A 35-year-old woman with social anxiety

1. Present (current situation):
The client has to express her opinion in a work meeting. Suddenly, she experiences palpitations, sweating, and muscle tension.

2. Past (early experiences):
As a child, when she gave the wrong answer in school, her teacher and classmates would make fun of her. This humiliating experience has been repeated many times.

3. Behavioral and emotional reactions (triangle output):
Emotional: Fear of judgment, shame, and worthlessness.
Behavioral: Remaining silent, avoiding speaking in public, blushing, lowering her head.

In general, the purpose of emotion-working exercises is to release and externalize emotions with the aim of reducing the emotional burden of previously repressed memories and discovering external and internal core constructers with the aim of becoming aware of the roots of personality formation and current abnormal behaviors, and moving from the level of emotion to the level of perception, with the aim of interrupting the vicious cycles of the past and growing and maturing the current personality.

Techniques for Discovering Internal Core Construct

As mentioned, inner structures refer to our desires, needs, and unspoken inner feelings and emotions from childhood to the present time, and are in fact a dialogue between the conscious and mature side of the individual (I) and the unconscious and childish side (Me). Technically and clinically, the same three categories of techniques are used, but with the aim of discovering inner structures (Johari Fard, 2024; 2025).

1. Questioning-Probing

Creating a deep dialogue with oneself and the inner child to reveal neglected needs. For example, the client can ask himself in a dialogue:

When I was a little child, what did I want most but no one gave it to me?

If my inner child could speak, what would it want from me now?

When did I feel most safe and at peace? Who or what provided it?

In the workbook, clients are provided with a table to discover their inner needs.

2. Patterning-Framing

Discover the historical or emotional origins and roots of these needs in the person's life. For example, you would ask the client:

Trace each discovered need: When was the first time I felt this need unmet?

What experience, relationship, or childhood event does this need go back to?

What emotion did I feel when this need went unmet (fear, anger, sadness)?

Here, a map of the emotional roots and history of the person's unmet needs and desires can be discovered.

3. Naming- Effecting

The unspoken, discovered needs and desires of the client can be named with his cooperation and then the effect of these dissatisfactions on his life can be examined. To help the client, the workbook contains exercises and examples.

□ Below we examine an example of the steps in applying excitement techniques.

Patient: There was a lot of difference between me and my older sister when I was a child. She had fair skin, colored eyes, and a beautiful face, and I had black eyes and hair, skin, and a normal appearance!

Therapist: Do you think a polarity was created between you and your sister? That is, you were at opposite and contradictory poles in most behaviors? (Questioning-Probing Technique)

Patient: Yes, exactly! For example, I was a student and my sister was not. I was more independent and my sister was dependent on the family. I was aggressive and my sister was passive and...

Therapist: Were these differences related to your later problems? For example, self-confidence? Or receiving attention from outside the home? (Patterning-Framing Technique)

Patient: Yes, I usually spent the whole day outside the home and kept myself busy with different classes. My self-confidence was so low that when someone said you were beautiful, I laughed at them and couldn't believe it.

Therapist: So a name was created for you in the family. By name? (Naming Technique)

Patient: "Ugly girl"!

Therapist: And its effects affected your behavioral and emotional reactions for years (Effecting Technique).

Chapter 8

Theoretical and Clinical Foundations of Perception Working

Chapter 8

Theoretical and Clinical Foundations of Perception-Working

The issue of perception in self-working is so important that the first self-working challenge in the chapter 5, entitled "On the Deception of Perception," addressed the impact of false perception on self-concept, reality testing, self-esteem/self-efficacy, decision-making, and the individual's life world in general.

In self-working, there is a close relationship between perception and narrative, and for this reason, this stage is considered as two complementary tasks, both perception and narrative. Vygotsky (2001) considers language as a mediator of thought that has a major impact on our representation of reality, and Bruner (1990) believes that the construction of reality has a narrative nature. Two parallel conceptual and metaphorical systems in the left and right hemispheres are responsible for structuring thoughts and ideas. We organize our experiences, memories, and memory based on narratives.

Past events in memory can be reprocessed by changing narratives from the traumatized child with limited processing capacity to the narrative of a healthy adult with greater capacity and experience, so that the individual's perception and feeling of the past can change. Many postmodern approaches in psychotherapy and second-type cybernetics, as well as the foundations of chaos theory, argue that reality can be changed by the smallest phenomena (such as semantic reframing techniques, the butterfly effect, etc.), which is very important and can change many of the patient's narratives of past traumas and correct his damaged way of perceiving today (Johari Fard, 2024; 2025).

Perception-Working/Narrative-Working Techniques

Perception creates concepts for us, and these concepts connect the external and strange world with our internal and personal world, and consequently, such a process, like a double-edged sword, can be both practical and useful for the individual, and ineffective and harmful. Because, the formation of a wrong concept will lead to a wrong understanding of many phenomena, and of course, such damage will be greater for abstract concepts such as freedom, progress, success, love, and the like. For example, if a person has had a wrong understanding of the concept of success since childhood, then he wants to be successful at all costs and may cause a lot of harm to himself and those around him in this way. Therefore, our perception of man, the world, and external events depends on our perceptual style, and in the words of postmodern philosophers, our narration of those events (narration).

In general, in this section, we want to strengthen self-awareness and work on perception, interpretation (from the perspective of traditional psychoanalysis) and our own perception style of past, present and future issues, with the narration of a healthy and developed adult.

Life can be considered as a story, of which you and I were not the authors. A story that began before birth, the marriage of parents in which I had no role, in a country, city, religion and culture that existed before us. We did not even have a role in the time, place and manner of our birth and more importantly, in the first years of life, when self-awareness had not yet formed, events occurred that had a great impact on the sense of safety and peace and the health of our body and mind in later years.

On the surface, the story is tragic and unpleasant; as if everything is in a forced and unwanted state. And as Maya Angelou said, ‘’there is no greater torment than to bear an untold story within yourself.” But the good news is that what makes our life narrative so unpleasant is the narrative of a vulnerable child who feels an immature perceptual style and limited psychological possibilities for change, whereas if we narrate the same life through the narrative of a healthy and mature adult, we can narrate and reprocess the unfortunate events of the past in a new way and find a new feeling for our past.

Renaming/Reframing Techniques

Renaming or renaming technique is a technique in which the client re-names their past naming and concepts, which originated from a childish perception, with a mature perception. This changes the perspective, reduces the negative emotional burden, and opens new paths for perception.

The most famous and widely used example in this field is the name and concept of perfectionism, which apparently wants to lead us to growth, progress, and perfection, but with a mature perception we realize that we are trapped in the trap of perfectionism, the tyranny of musts and strict standards, and this is not perfectionism. So we find a new and mature name and definition for it that eliminates the harmful aspects of perfectionism and only keeps the aspect of growth and perfection.

The technique of reframing, in harmony with the technique of redefinition, also deals with the creation of a new and mature narrative and perception of concepts, memories, events and behaviors, and gradually frees the individual from a childish perception of himself and life, and indeed the past. One of the very useful techniques for practicing narrative in the Self-Working Workbook is the Switch Exercise.

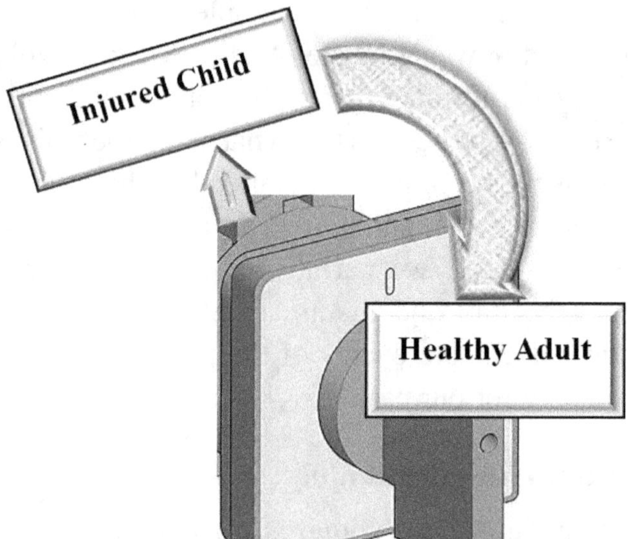

Figure 8.1 Switch Exercise. Switch from Past Narrative (Injured Child) to Present Narrative (Healthy Adult)

Any event may seem painful and catastrophic through the lens of a traumatized child's narrative: a parent's fight, a mother's threat to leave home, failing an exam, a teacher's punishment, etc. However, when it is addressed 20 to 30 years later and through the lens of a healthy adult's narrative, with different biological, psychological, and social circumstances and generally more life experience, a new perception and understanding is formed that reduces the traumatic effects of the past. The following is an example of narrative and perceptual style change with the help of redefinition, reframing, and switching techniques.

Behbod, 38, a senior expert in an industrial company and single, diagnosed with depression, after numerous sessions on emotion-working and narrative-working, described his two narratives in relation to his father as follows:

A narrative of a damaged child (Behbood, 8 years old): My father criticized me since childhood and would pick on me about everything. He would say, “Sit down, study, why did you say that to so-and-so?” He never approved of me and looked at my work with a mocking eye. Although I was his only child who studied and as a senior engineer, I have a good job, I still don’t see myself in his eyes.

A narrative of a healthy adult (38-year-old Behbood): Now that I look back at my father’s behavior at my age, I realize that he loved me very much and did not want my fate to be like that of my other brothers and sisters, and he thought that with these constant nagging and reminders, I would make more progress. Of course, his method was wrong, but with his knowledge and old-fashioned upbringing style, this was the best he knew how to do. This way of narrating my father’s behavior has changed many of the anger and resentment I felt towards him, and I feel like I can forgive him and let go of his words and behavior.

Chapter 9

Theoretical and Clinical Foundations of Attention-Working

Chapter 9

Theoretical and Clinical Foundations of Attention-Working

Attention is a cognitive ability that refers to the active processing, selection, and focus on a stimulus. Cognitive theorists believe that attention to obtain factual information is the first step in the formation of healthy behaviors, and in the field of self-regulation, attention and awareness are the main focus of maintaining and enhancing psychological functioning. Also, in cybernetic theories, attention is key to communication and control processes and is thought to underlie behavior regulation. Many cognitive psychology articles consider attention bias to threatening stimuli as a cause of anxiety, to negative memories of the past as a cause of depression, and also to other traumatic stimuli as a cause of other psychological disorders.

Also, biofeedback research considers attention as a central element in reducing unhealthy physical conditions or symptoms of disease. Dysregulation of emotions and behaviors occurs when symptoms, cues, and triggers are ignored or suppressed and not paid attention to (for example, when a person uses alcohol, painkillers, medication, etc.).

Mindfulness in self-working means cultivating and training attention, it means working with attention in a conscious, mature, responsible, and creative way. Therefore, at this stage, mindfulness exercises are performed, as well as paying mature attention to stimuli and examining the effects of these attention practices on life (life). In other words, mindfulness in self-working emphasizes more on the conscious guidance of attention (Johari Fard, 2024).

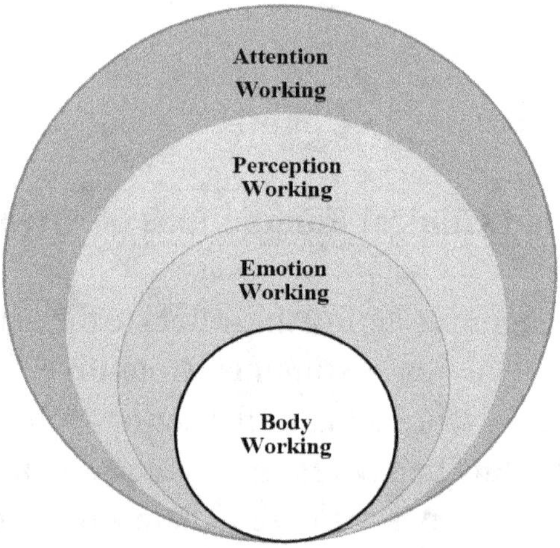

Figure 9.1 The Hierarchy of the Stages of Rationality (Johari Fard, 2024; 2025).

Attention is the highest process of the human psyche and can cover the body-emotion-perception hierarchy. Attention to the body, attention to emotion, attention to perception! Why, despite the importance of attention to perception, emotion and the body, do we work on this being at the end? Unlike some therapeutic perspectives such as mindfulness and acceptance and commitment therapy, which work on attention from the beginning, and leave many of the person's past physical, emotional and perceptual issues unresolved, in self-working, this part of the treatment occurs in the fourth step and after working with the lower parts. In fact, at this stage, the person can separate himself from the lower levels of the brain and find the readiness to use attention in everyday life in a conscious, mature, responsible, and creative way (Johari Fard, 2024).

Theoretical Foundations of Attention

1. Neuroscience foundations neural networks related to attention include:

   1.1 Neural network for focused and selective attention (Executive Control Network)

   1.2 Neural network for shifting attention to important stimuli (Salience Network)

   1.3 Neural network for internal attention and self-awareness (Default Mode Network)

   Attention-working can cause measurable changes in the prefrontal cortex, parietal cortex, and inter-network connectivity (Tang et al., 2015).

2. Cognitive Psychology Foundations

2.1 Attention Resource Theory (Kahneman, 1973)

Attention is a limited resource and the way it is allocated determines the quality of information processing and decision-making, such as selective, sustained, and shifting attention. Attention-working can improve all three types of attention, which plays a role in reducing distraction and increasing efficiency.

2.2 Broadbent's Filter Model

The mind filters and screens incoming stimuli and processes only what is in line with goals.

3. Third Generation of Behavioral Therapies (Mindfulness-based Psychotherapy)

3.1 Mindfulness-Based Interventions

According to Jon Kabat-Zinn's research, mindfulness practices reduce anxiety, depression, and increase self-regulation.

3.2 Acceptance and Commitment Therapy (ACT)

Paying attention to thoughts, emotions, and body, without judgment, to create psychological distance and choose behavior that is aligned with values.

4. Attention in the Self-Working Model

In the self-working model, attention is the fourth level of the four-level brain, the training of which can direct attention on the levels of perception-emotion-body in a conscious, mature, responsible, and creative manner. Attention acts as a ''monitoring system'' that receives data from the body, emotion, and perception and decides in the moment where to focus. From this perspective, attention is not just an individual skill, but a regulatory process of the entire body-mind system.

Attention and Gratitude

One of the best ways to pay attention and consciously, maturely, responsibly, and creatively direct attention is gratitude. Attention, if consciously directed, can shift attention from non-existents to existing things; from ugliness to beauty; from deficiencies to being; and be grateful for existing things and possessions. Gratitude increases our attention to our possessions and, instead of focusing on what one does not have and what does not exist, it guides us to consciously feeling of what exists (Johari Fard, 2024).

The fMRI studies show that the experience of gratitude is associated with activation of the medial prefrontal cortex (mPFC), anterior cingulate cortex (ACC), and amygdala (Kinney et al., 2016). It also activates the brain's reward system in areas such as the ventral striatum and nucleus accumbens, which are associated with pleasure and motivation.

In Stoic philosophy, gratitude is presented as a form of awareness of what one has and acceptance of the world as it is, a source of peace. In Kantian ethics, gratitude is a moral duty and a response to the benevolence of others. In the existentialist perspective, gratitude is part of ''responsible acceptance of life'' and finding meaning in everyday experiences. And in spiritual psychology, gratitude is a bridge between the self and the ''other'' (human, nature, or the transcendent), which strengthens a sense of connection and empathy.

Chapter 10

Theoretical and Clinical Foundations of Future-Working

Chapter 10

Theoretical and Clinical Foundations of Future-Working

The second part of self-working is ''Becoming-to-That" which is also called future-working. Future-working means working consciously, maturely, responsibly, and creatively with the future. In fact, as opposed to working on the past, it is also important to work on the future. Many therapeutic approaches, including psychoanalysis, after finishing the analysis and observing signs of ego strengthening, psychological growth and personality maturation and increased reality testing, they end the treatment and leave the rest of life up to the individual. On the other hand, humanistic therapists, especially Rogerian ones, and recently in some third-generation approaches, emphasize solely on the positive aspects of the personality (resources), values clarification, and commitment to values (action), without considering the individual's past and traumas.

In my opinion, as a clinical psychotherapist dealing with a patient with a disorder, each of these approaches considers one side of the psyche and does not have a holistic and systems-based view of the human being (like yin without yang). In other words, in self-working, we first solve the problem of the individual with the past and then, passing through the path of body-emotion-perception-attention, we deal with the individual's future and the creation of what he wants. And as mentioned in the seven moments of self-working, we set the rhythm of life on the two beats of acceptance (what we are; on this being) and creation (what we want; becoming).

This idea may sound familiar and evoke humanistic or acceptance and commitment (ACT) theories, but what is noteworthy is the very adventurous path and the many sessions of working on the past that are not worked on in these treatments. In other words, we have balanced and regulated the excessive pessimism of psychoanalysis with the excessive optimism of humanism.

The second part of self-working, namely working with the future (future-building) and the process of its creation, is influenced by the approaches of Allport, Rogers, Maslow, Steven Hayes, and even Adler. For this purpose, we enter from three paths: first, examining the ideal self and comparing it with the real self, second, discovering the positive aspects of the personality (resources) and retelling the past and personality with the aim of discovering these characteristics, and third, finding values.

In general, the stage of becoming consists of four parts (Johari Fard, 2024; 2025):

1. Ideal self
2. Resources
3. Life values
4. Its creation

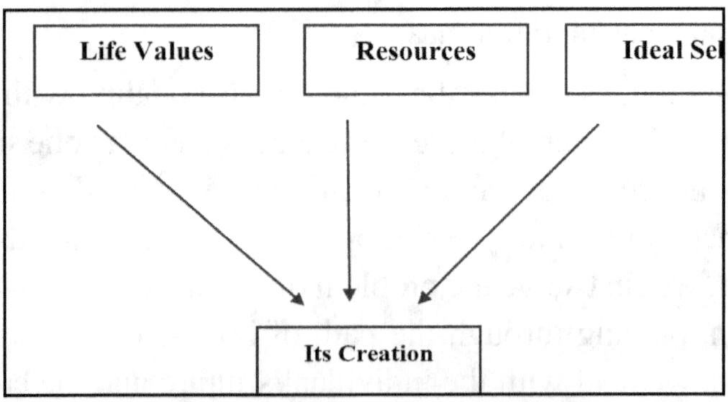

Figure 10.1 Becoming-to-That (Future-Working); Its Parts And Techniques (Johari Fard, 2024; 2025)

Theoretical foundations of Becoming (Future-Working)

Thetheoreticalfoundationsof"future-working"canbeformulated with a combination of positive psychology, motivational, and personal growth theories.

1. Foundations of Developmental Psychology and Motivation

1.1 Self-Determination Theory (Deci & Ryan): It emphasizes the basic psychological needs (autonomy, competence, relatedness) that are essential for mapping and pursuing the future.

2.1 Goal-Setting Theory (Locke & Latham): Future-working improves performance and motivation by setting specific, challenging, and meaningful goals.

3.1 Snyder's Hope Theory: Future-working requires two key elements: pathways thinking and agency thinking. And future-working has both the elements of pathway-making and agency.

2. Foundations of Positive Psychology

1.2 Eudaimonic Well-being Model (Ryff): Future-working is directly related to creating meaning, personal growth, and mastery over the environment.

2.2 Psychological Capital Theory (Luthans): The four components of hope, optimism, resilience, and self-efficacy provide the psychological infrastructure for future-oriented thinking.

3.2 Strengths-Based Approaches: Focus on discovering strengths, abilities, and values in order to design the future and future-working.

3. Foundations of Futures Studies and Systems Thinking

1.3 Scenario Planning (Schoemaker): Futures-working relies on diverse and flexible scenarios rather than linear predictions.

2.3 Complexity and Chaos Theory: The future is not completely predictable; flexibility, self-organization, and readiness for nonlinear changes are essential. Sometimes a small change (the butterfly effect) can create big changes in the future.

3.3 Systems Thinking (Senge): Understanding the relationships between the components of life and their interactions on the path to the future.

Chapter 11

Theoretical and Clinical Foundations of Life-Working

Chapter 11

Theoretical and Clinical Foundations of Life-Working

The third part of self-working is called the "Life-Theme", which begins with the title of living or working consciously, maturely, responsibly, and creatively with life. If we consider the first stage of self-working (Being-on-This) as working with the past (past-working), and the second stage of self-working (Becoming-to-That) as working with the future (future-working), the third stage is working with the present, or so-called now and here.

This section is designed to work with life in the present (living), but it also teaches self-working action. Self-working action means doing anything (working) in a conscious, mature, responsible, and creative way (Johari Fard, 2024; 2025):

Body-working (conscious, mature, responsible, and creative care of the body),

Emotion-working (conscious, mature, responsible, and creative care of emotion),

Perception-working (conscious, mature, responsible, and creative care of perception),

Attention-working (conscious, mature, responsible, and creative care of attention),

Future-working (conscious, mature, responsible, and creative care of the future).

The third part of self-working, if the previous two parts are done well, can guarantee the implementation and actions of the individual in the path of life, and as mentioned, the four main characteristics of discipline, namely living with a conscious theme, living with a mature theme, living with a responsible theme and living with a creative theme, are carried out here through specific exercises and therapeutic stages.

An interesting and noteworthy point from the numerous reports of clients is that many unresolved and traumatic issues of the individual's past, as well as concerns and confusions about his future, are no longer raised and in therapy sessions, the focus can be on the individual's movement in the path of life.

Theoretical Foundations of Life Theme

The concept of life theme consists of two parts, which include life schema and life path. Life schema is the mental plan and framework of an individual towards life; a specific type of mentality of an individual towards external issues. In fact, it is the intersubjective dimension of life. Life schema must be placed in a life path in order to manifest. Life path is the objective and external dimension of life (intersubjective), which has direction and, like a vector, moves our life in a certain direction.

1. Life Schema: The Mental and Internal Dimension of the Life Theme

A life schema is a set of beliefs, mental images, memories, values, and expectations that an individual has in their mind about ''how to live" and presence in life." This section is aligned with the following theories:

1.1 Jeffrey Young's Schema Theory: Stable cognitive-emotional structures in the mind.
1.2 Marcus and Norris's Possible Selves Theory: Images of the desirable self, the fearful self, and the possible self.

1.3 Meaning in Life Patterns: Attention to long-term goals and values as a guiding framework.

2. Life Path: The External and Objective Dimension of the Life Theme

The life path represents the practical and external embodiment of the life theme in the real world; it includes the choices, situations, relationships, achievements and experiences that are formed over time. This section is aligned with the following theories:

2.1 Erik Erikson's Life Cycle Approach (Psychosocial Stages): Developmental transitions and crises of each stage.

2.2 Life Course Theory: The role of historical, social and cultural factors in the formation of the life path.

2.3 Positive Psychology: Focus on strengths, flourishing and achieving meaningful goals.

Life theme is the set of life schema and life path. When our life moves in a specific direction with a framework and internal-external boundaries, the life theme is actually in doubt. Life theme is a path of growth and transformation in the direction of becoming! (Becoming) If we liken life to a journey that has a specific origin and destination, then the path between the origin and destination can be called the "life path", and the mental plan of the journey is the "life schema" and these two together create our "life theme".

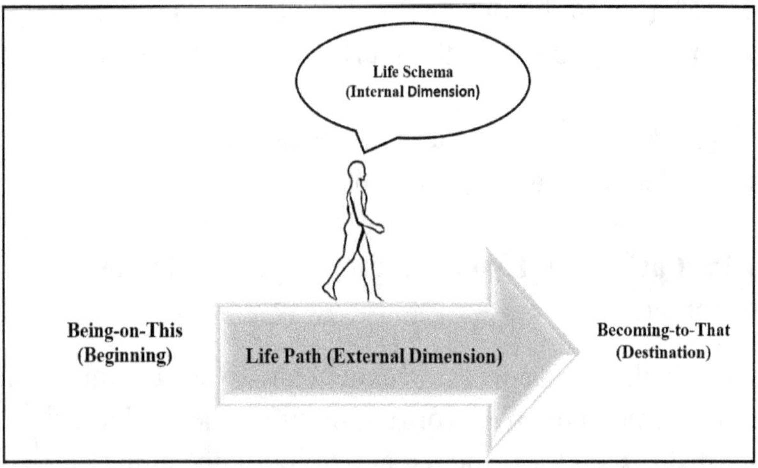

Figure 11.1 Formation of the Life Theme . The Life Theme is formed from the interaction and interaction of the intra-mental dimension of "life schema" and the extra-mental dimension of "life path", which is formed from a source of perception of Being-on-This (Beginning) and the purpose of its creation Becoming-to-That (Destination) (Johari Fard, 2024).

In general, the life schema is the mental guidance and interpretation of the life theme and life path, the implementation of the life schema, and the examination of real feedback in the context of life. And this continuous interaction shapes the life theme and turns it into a living, flexible, and reproducible experience.

The Four Themes of Life (Self-Working Action)

The self-working person, on the path of his life, from the beginning of "on this being" to the destination of "becoming", must cultivate and coordinate (balance) the four aspects of his life theme like the four wheels of a car. These four aspects include (Joharifard, 2024; 2025):

1. Living with a conscious theme
2. Living with a mature theme
3. Living with a responsible theme
4. Living with a creative theme

Self-working action means considering the conscious, mature, responsible and creative dimensions in every action of life. Recognizing each of these dimensions can help maintain mental health in the path of life. The four themes of life, with each of its sub-quadrants, like a framework and scaffolding, keep your life on the path of life and move you on the path of growth and self-realization.

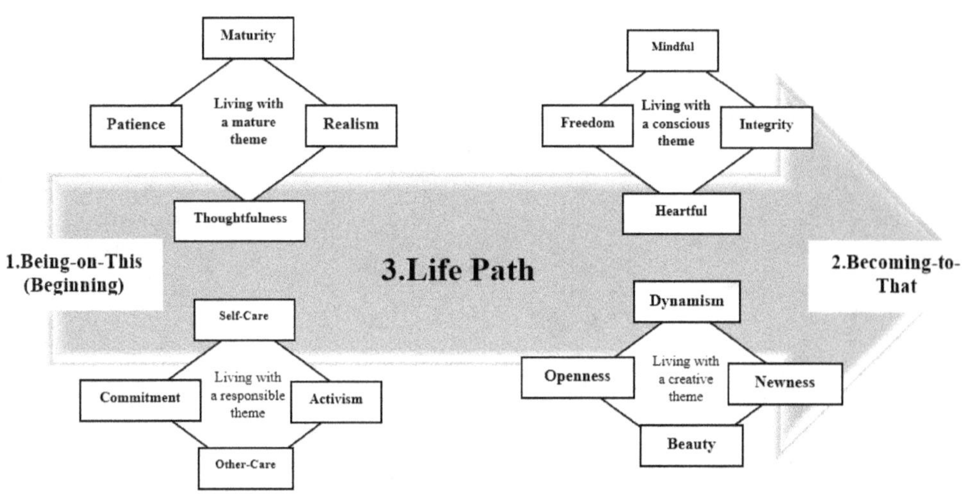

Figure 11.2 Four Themes of Life (Self-Working Action) (Johari Fard, 2024; 2025).

Chapter 12

Research in Self-Working

Chapter 12
Research in Self-Working

Self-working has been based on clinical and experimental research since its early days, and this research path continues. In general, self-working research is conducted in two ways: qualitative and quantitative.

Qualitative Research in Self-Efficacy

In qualitative research, the goal is to discover the lived experiences of clients and therapists of the self-efficacy process. The self-efficacy workbook introduces many examples of clients' lived experiences. The data collection tools in these studies are semi-structured in-depth interviews, analysis of treatment notes, and participant observation in sessions. Fortunately, clients have been very cooperative in this regard and have so far provided me and the self-efficacy research team with their in-depth and practical notes. The following is a qualitative research model with the cooperation and consent of the clients:

The Case of Prima[1]

Prima was a 33-year-old woman with a master's degree, married and childless. She was initially diagnosed with anxiety disorders, severe obsessive-compulsive disorder, and sometimes

1- She is much appreciated for willingly providing me with detailed reports of her treatment and self-working.

experienced dissociative states due to high anxiety. Given the lack of success in drug treatments and behavioral and cognitive training, she was offered self-working therapy upon requesting psychoanalysis.

Body-Working

The first stage of self-working was physical exercise. Due to her strange and anxiety-provoking dissociative states, Prima avoided any physical exercise and had a strong resistance to connecting with her body. However, she cautiously began brief exercises in the field of body awareness and relaxation and body-working such as massage, aerobic exercises, physical training (body care) and especially self-expression training, which took several months to achieve satisfactory results. At this stage, she was advised to do physical exercises as part of her lifestyle, on a daily basis. The results of these exercises reduced anxiety and the dissociative states that resulted from them and improved communication with her body.

Emotion-Working

The part of working with trauma and past memories was progressing very slowly due to Prima's resistance. At this stage, first, exercises were done to release and connect with the emotional part of the personality, and gradually we moved towards externalizing and expressing the repressed traumas.

Some of his traumatic memories, such as the birth of his younger sister a year later (and his mother's lack of adequate care), his father's very strict and controlling behavior towards his mother (including constant arguments and fights between his parents), living with a schizophrenic uncle and seeing his strange behavior (his uncle's pessimism, fights, and beatings), being humiliated and rejected by his friends during his school years, etc., led to the discovery of his external triggers, and with the help of excitement techniques (such as questioning-probing; patterning-framing; naming-effecting), a core maker was discovered and named "the elixir of peace." Of course, other core makers were also discovered and named, and with the help of the triangle of effecting, their impact on his life was examined. In the section on discovering internal core makers, meeting and talking with his childhood and examining needs led to the discovery of the need for progress and support from others.

Perception-Working

Prima's change in narrative and perceptual style, at this age and with that amount of traumatic memories, was initially strange and unbelievable to her. However, gradually, by understanding the concept of "narrative" and becoming familiar with the postmodern perspective (soft and changeable reality), and perceptual techniques (such as renaming and reframing), she was able to gain a new perspective on life from the perspective of a healthy adult.

Attention-Working

In complete disbelief, Prima was able to say goodbye to the past (break from the past) and consciously bring her attention to her present possessions (being aware) and gradually become grateful for what she had.

The Second Stage of Self-Working: Becoming-to-That (Future-Working)

Ideal Self

In the initial interview form, Prima described herself as selfish, nervous, impatient, obsessive, intolerant, hardworking, etc. At this stage, she introduced characteristics such as kindness, calmness, stability, generosity, patience, and the like as her ideal self.

Resources

By examining the potential and actual talents of her parents, as well as examining her own strengths in the past, she had discovered characteristics such as high intelligence and analytical power, writing, leadership, being a reader, and hardworking.

Values

Study and learning, physical health and especially personal growth were Prima's most important values.

Creating it

In the creation session, the sum of the discussion and consideration of the ideal self, talents and values led to the creation and construction of the future and the formation of the horizon of life.

The third Stage of Self-Working: Life Theme

Life schema

Prima now had a clear plan for her life. A past that she was aware of and a future designed from the characteristics of her personality.

Living with a Conscious Theme

In her notes, Prima explained the experience of increasing her awareness and consciousness in life and especially found unity suitable for her fragmented and restless personality. Also, the practice of freedom freed her from the shackles of past beliefs: "I see myself as a bright point that is full of awareness... a bright point in this infinite world... I am light, and free... I am full of love... I am in the moment..."

Living with an Adult Theme

From Prima's perspective, the weakest part of her personality was her adult self, and she practiced this part with great seriousness. In practicing realism, she noticed the imbalance between her imaginary and real life: "When I see what I want in my imagination, it's great. Everything goes the way I want it to. I create scenarios in my mind... There are no limits... I enjoy it... There are no frameworks... But when I return to the real world, I experience failure. Here, I am not the one who sets the rules... Reality has boundaries and you have to follow them, and this is difficult... Sometimes it is difficult to distinguish the boundary between reality and fantasy and it confuses me... Now, through self-working exercises, I have learned that reality is not absolute and that it is possible to move forward with it through the method of acceptance-creation... In sessions with Dr. Joharifard, we worked a lot on this issue and I failed many times... But, I tried to continue stronger..."

Living with a Responsible Theme

Practicing self-care and other-care taught Prima a balance between caring for herself and others: ''Now, with self-care practices, I am kinder to myself, I am more comfortable dealing with my own shortcomings and forgiving, I expect less from myself and, consequently, I expect less from others... I have reduced my expectations of others... I have recognized my own capacity."

With the practice of activism, she behaved consciously, maturely, and responsibly, and felt useful, valuable, and powerful.

Living with a Creative Theme

Prima is currently undergoing this part of the treatment, and the feeling of dynamism in life and openness to new experiences in the real world is very practical and attractive to her.

Quantitative Research in Self-Working

In quantitative research, the goal is to test the effectiveness of self-discipline educational and therapeutic protocols and examine variables. In this context, descriptive and inferential statistical methods such as multi-way analysis of variance, multi-way analysis of covariance, and the like have been used in theses and scientific articles. Theses conducted at the master's degree level in clinical psychology include:

1. The effectiveness of the self-working educational and therapeutic program on quality of life, psychological flexibility, and psychological well-being in female university students (Student: Saeed Rangin Kaman).

2. The effectiveness of the self-working educational and therapeutic program on emotional self-regulation, self-efficacy in diabetes management, and cognitive flexibility in patients with type 2 diabetes at Golestan Hospital, Ahvaz (Student: Negin Musavat).

3. The effectiveness of the self-working educational and therapeutic program on self-criticism, internalized shame, and perfectionism of students (Student: Zahra Nawaser).

4. The effectiveness of the self-working educational therapy program on self-efficacy, body image, perceived stress and mentalization in adolescents with anxiety (Student: Elaheh Khojastehpour).

5. The effectiveness of the self-working educational therapy program on self-perception, meaning of life and existential anxiety in those referred to psychology clinics in Ahvaz (Student: Atefeh Sarkheh).

6. The effectiveness of the self- working educational therapy program on attachment style, ego strength and defense mechanisms in students with depression (Student: Zahra Nikoei Borujeni).

7. The effectiveness of the self-working educational therapy program on resilience, self-efficacy and emotional self-awareness in married students (Student: Mahdieh Zalghi).

8. The effectiveness of the self-working educational therapy program on self-efficacy, adaptability and self-criticism in female students (Student: Mina Atofat).

9. The effectiveness of the self-working educational therapy program on resilience, psychological flexibility and hope in women with depression referring to psychological clinics (Student: Sedighe Khajovi).

10. The effectiveness of the self- working educational therapy program on psychological well-being, resilience and self-confidence of students at Farhangian University (Student: Morteza Alizadeh).

Appendices

Self-Working Interview Form

By: Reza Johari Fard

The purpose of this interview form is to gain a comprehensive and clear picture of your life. As explained in the book, self-working is an approach to finding your life path, to free yourself from life confusion and unconscious decisions. By completing these questions, you will avoid wasting time in self-working sessions. For your safety, we must remind you that this information will remain completely confidential and will be kept with the therapist.

1. Write down the positive and negative traits of your personality during childhood and adolescence from your own perspective.

2. Write down the positive and negative traits of your personality during childhood and adolescence from the perspective of others.

3. List your painful childhood memories.

4. List your painful teenage memories.

5. List your father's characteristics when you were a child and teenager.

6. List your mother's characteristics when you were a child and teenager.

7. Who were the other important people in your life, and how did they influence you?

8. Who was your role model when you were a child and teenager?

9. In your opinion, which of your needs were not satisfied in the past?

10. What were your dreams and ideals in the past?

11. What are your plans for the future?

Self-Working Research Protocol

The Self-Working Research Protocol is designed for use in academic and clinical research. The table below shows how many sessions of this protocol.

Sessions	Contents
First	Introduction and familiarity with the norms and rules of the group, the seven stages of self-working
Second	Part 1. Treatment (on this being), physical changes (body-working); relaxation exercises, body training, body awareness
Third	Emotional changes (emotion-working); releasing, externalization
Fourth	Emotional changes (emotion-working); imagery, letter writing

Source: Joharifard, Reza (2024). Self-Working Therapy Training Program. Tehran: Danjeh Publications.

The use of this therapy protocol for research, thesis or article is subject to written permission from the author. The use of this therapy requires training and its implementation must be carried out under the supervision of a supervisor.

Please send your request to rjoharifard@gmail.com.
Website: www.selfworking.org

Questions and Answers about Self-Working

1. Question: What disorders is self-working suitable for?

Answer: Self-working is a transdiagnostic method; a therapeutic model for examining and repairing the root and cause of disorders. Therefore, it can be used for all mental disorders.

2. Question: When is self-working recommended in clinical work?

Answer: Based on the systems thinking model, conduct the first session as a diagnostic interview (without an approach and with the aim of diagnosing the disorder based on DSM) and the next session as a therapeutic interview (based on the choice of a therapeutic approach and with the aim of formulating the disorder). Since self-working is considered an in-depth approach to disorders, it is better to first reduce the individual's signs and symptoms through medication and behavioral and cognitive exercises and then enter self- working.

3. Question: How long does self- working last?

Answer: The stages and process of self- working are completely defined and clear and can vary depending on the individual's circumstances. For example, for some clients, physical exercises take too long, and for others, they are exciting, etc. It is better to perform the self-working stages carefully and patiently, and not to rush to achieve the result and end the treatment. Self- working has a dynamic nature and it is recommended to always be in the individual's lifestyle.

4. Question: From what age can self- working be applied? Can it be used for children?

Answer: Currently, self- working is applied to adults and the appropriate protocol for children has not been studied.

5. Question: Can self-working be implemented in a group?

Answer: Yes. Various self- working groups have already been formed and satisfactory results are being reported.

6. Question: What are the stages of self-training training for therapists?

Answer: Clinical therapists who are familiar with the principles of psychopathology and clinical psychology and psychotherapy, after passing theoretical and practical workshops in the field of self- working, reviewing and studying client reports, can implement self- working under the supervision of a supervisor.

7. Question: Is self- working useful for healthy people?

Answer: Self-working means training the personality; therefore, its implementation can be implemented in superficial to deep layers (depending on the type of problem). Self- working for healthy people, without engaging with deep parts of the personality and traumatic memories, can help improve the lifestyle of all people.

References:

Alexander, L. (197). *Bioenergetic psychotherapy.* Retrieved from https://openlibrary.org/books/OL24745085M/ Bioenergetics

Amir, N., Elias, J., Klumpp, H., & Przeworski, A. (2003). Attentional bias to threat in social phobia: Facilitated processing of threat or difficulty disengaging attention from threat? *Behaviour Research and Therapy, 41,* 1325–1335.

Body Psychotherapy. (n.d.). Retrieved from http://www.europsyche.org/contents/13215/body-psychotherapy

Bruner, J. (1990). *Acts of meaning. Cambridge*, MA: Harvard University Press.

Bruner, J. (2002). *Making stories: Law, literature, life*. New York: Farrar, Straus & Giroux.

Bruner, J. (2003). The narrative construction of reality. In *Narrative Intelligence.* Philadelphia: John Benjamins Publishing Company.

Carlson, N., & Birkett, M. (2017). *Physiology of behavior.* New York: Pearson.

Carlson, N. (2014). *Foundations of behavioral neuroscience.* New York: Pearson.

Dalgleish, T., Moradi, A. R., Taghavi, R., Neshat-Doost, H. T., Yule, W., & Canterbury, R. (2000). Judgments about emotional events in children and adolescents with post-traumatic stress disorder and controls. Journal of Child Psychology and Psychiatry, 41, 981–988.

Dalgleish, T., Taghavi, R., Neshat-Doost, H., Moradi, A., Canterbury, R., & Yule, W. (2003). Patterns of processing bias for emotional information across clinical disorders: A comparison of attention, memory, and prospective cognition in children and adolescents with depression, generalized anxiety, and posttraumatic stress disorder. *Journal of Clinical Child and Adolescent Psychology, 32*, 10–21.

Derryberry, D., & Reed, M. (2002). Anxiety-related attentional biases and their regulation by attentional control. *Journal of Abnormal Psychology, 111,* 225–236.

Di Chiara, G. (2000). Role of dopamine in the behavioral actions of nicotine related to addiction. *European Journal of Pharmacology.*

Eddy, M. (2009). A brief history of somatic practices and dance: Historical development of the field of somatic education and its relationship to dance. *Journal of Dance & Somatic Practices.*

Ehrenreich, J. T., & Gross, A. M. (2002). Biased attentional behavior in childhood anxiety: A review of theory and current empirical investigation. *Clinical Psychology Review, 22*, 991–1008.

Field, M. (2004). Cognitive bias and drug craving in recreational cannabis users. *Drug and Alcohol Dependence.*

Ingram, N. (2009). *The international encyclopedia of depression.* New York: Springer Publishing Company.

Johari Fard, R. (2024). *Psychotherapeutic techniques based on approaches and methods* (6th ed.). Tehran: Dehkadeh Salamat Publications.

Johari Fard, R. (2024). *Self-working therapeutic educational program.* Tehran: Danjeh Publications.

Johari Fard, R. (2024). *Self-working therapeutic educational program (workbook)*. Tehran: Ravanshani and Honar Publications.

Johari Fard, R. (2025). Self-working: A novel integrative approach to psychotherapy. In IV. *International British Congress on Interdisciplinary Scientific Research & Practices.* London, UK.

Leahy, R. L. (2018). *Emotional schema therapy.* Guilford Press.

Ma, X., et al. (2017). The effect of diaphragmatic breathing on attention, negative affect and stress in healthy adults. *Frontiers in Psychology.*

Miller, A., & Jenkins, A. (2006). *The body never lies: The lingering effects of hurtful parenting.* W.W. Norton & Company.

Preece, D. A., Becerra, R., Robinson, K., & Gross, J. J. (2020).

he Emotion Regulation Questionnaire: Psychometric properties in general community samples. *Journal of Personality Assessment, 102*(3), 348–356. https://doi.org/10.1080/00223891.2018.1564319
Price, C. J., & Thompson, E. A. (2007). Measuring dimensions of body connection: Body awareness and bodily dissociation. *Journal of Alternative and Complementary Medicine.*

Robbins, D. (2001). *Vygotsky's psychology–philosophy: A metaphor for language theory and learning.* New York: Kluwer Academic/Plenum Publishers.

Sheehan, J. (1995). *Psychology as narrative: A critical application of Paul Ricoeur's philosophy of narrative to psychotherapy.* Dublin: University Press.

Teasdale, J. D., Segal, Z., & Williams, J. M. G. (1995). How does cognitive therapy prevent depressive relapse and why should attentional control (mindfulness) training help? *Behaviour Research and Therapy, 33*, 25–39.

Thielen, M. (2013). Body psychotherapy for anxiety disorders. *International Body Psychotherapy Journal, 13*(2), 44–60. Retrieved from http://usabp.org/wp-content/uploads/2013/10/IBPJ-volume-13-No2Fall2014.pdf

Totton, N. (2003). *Body psychotherapy: An introduction.* Maidenhead, England: Open University Press.

Utay, J. M., & Miller, M. (2006). Guided imagery as an effective therapeutic technique. *Journal of Instructional Psychology.*

Young, C. (1997). History of body psychotherapy. Retrieved from http://usabp.org/about-us/history-of-body-psychotherapy

www.ingramcontent.com/pod-product-compliance
Lightning Source LLC
LaVergne TN
LVHW022227200926
848481LV00006B/2160
9781778923203